I0458815

ALWAYS
BE LEARNING

THE PURSUIT OF KNOWLEDGE IN A WORLD THAT HAS FORGOTTEN ITS POWER

By
CHASE POWELL

Copyright Page

ALWAYS BE LEARNING
The Pursuit of Knowledge in a World That Has Forgotten Its Power

ISBN: **978-1-960410-20-7**

Printed in the United States of America
First Edition

Author Website: https://abl.codetap.ai

CONTENTS

The Calling
to Grow

"The mind once stretched by a new idea
never returns to its original dimensions."

— Oliver Wendell Holmes

L earning has never been easier to access, yet harder to truly practice. It's a strange contradiction of our time. We're surrounded by more information than any generation before us, and somehow we still find ourselves looking up trivial things—like whether expired yogurt is going to kill us. People scroll. They skim. They drift. The problem isn't intelligence or availability; it's that we've forgotten what it feels like to pursue understanding with intention.

The world around us has been engineered—quietly, steadily—to dull the mind. Everything aims at stimulation, convenience, or comfort. Entertainment dresses itself up as education. Constant noise becomes the default atmosphere. In a place like that, the ability to slow down, wrestle with an idea, examine a belief, or rebuild the interior of your thinking becomes rare. And because it's rare, it becomes powerful.

Learning has always been the quiet multiplier behind any kind of excellence, but today it carries even more weight.

I didn't arrive at that conviction suddenly. There was no single mountaintop moment. It came from years of reading men like Zig Ziglar, Stephen Covey, and Matthew Kelly—years of raising a family, running businesses, and being humbled by mistakes I didn't see coming. Over time, a pattern kept showing up: whenever I grew, learning sat at the front of the story. Whenever I stalled, something else had taken its place —distraction, ego, or simple comfort.

When attention splinters, identity starts to loosen.
When distraction takes the wheel, purpose fades.
When comfort becomes the baseline, discipline begins to look unreasonable.

But the inverse is just as true. Someone who chooses to learn—honestly, deliberately, and without pretending they already know—inevitably outgrows the boundaries that once held them in place.

This book is an attempt to restore the identity of the learner. Not with tricks or shortcuts, and not with motivational fireworks that burn out by the weekend. The aim is much older: discipline, purpose, reflection, and wisdom. The work of becoming someone is formed rather than scattered.

We'll start by looking directly at the forces shaping the modern mind— and then build a structure strong enough to resist them. I call that structure the Learner's Operating System (L-OS). It moves from the inside out:

• **Part I** looks at the cultural forces—comfort, overstimulation, and dopamine—quietly weakening the will.
• **Part II** focuses on the virtues that stabilize the interior life—humility, purpose, and self-talk.
• **Parts III through VII** lay down the practical playbook: meta-learning,

the Anti-Schedule, the thoughtful use of AI, and the discipline of saying no.

Learning is not just data collection. It shapes character. It orients the spirit. It strengthens the mind. It forms identity. It repairs meaning. This book is written for anyone who feels the distance between who they are and who they could be—and wants to close that distance with clarity rather than chaos.

Learning is the discipline of becoming.
And this moment in history may need that discipline more than any before it.

PART

I

THE MODERN CONDITION

We live in an age of unprecedented comfort, overstimulation, and distraction. The modern environment is engineered to pull attention outward, weaken discipline, and sedate ambition. Most people drift through life reacting rather than thinking—scrolling rather than learning, consuming rather than becoming. This part exposes the cultural forces that quietly erode identity, meaning, and mental strength.

Comfort becomes an addiction. Noise becomes normal. Attention becomes fragmented. And dopamine — the fuel of motivation — is burned out by constant micro-hits of entertainment. In this environment, the mind becomes fragile, reactive, and untrained.

Yet hidden inside this cultural decay lies an extraordinary advantage: anyone who chooses disciplined learning immediately separates from the masses. The world is full of soft minds and distracted lives. Depth is rare. Focus is rare. Curiosity is rare. Discipline is rare.

Part I frames both the crisis and the opportunity. It reveals why learning becomes identity, why formation becomes rebellion, and why the disciplined learner rises while others remain stuck. It establishes the foundation for the rest of the book: the problem isn't capability — it's environment. And the solution begins by rejecting drift.

If you want a preview of what the ultimate failure of attention looks like, watch the movie Idiocracy. It's a comedy that no longer feels like a comedy. The film's most terrifying insight is that the future doesn't belong to the wicked or the malicious; it belongs to the distracted. It is a world where all depth has been replaced by noise, and the most dangerous crime is simply thinking too hard.

The Forgotten Advantage: Learning as Identity

"You are what you are, and you are where you are because of what has gone into your mind."

— Zig Ziglar

Learning is not a technique; it is a declaration of identity. It used to be a way of life, shaping men and women from the inside out—forming character, sharpening purpose, and anchoring identity. Today, the world treats learning as an optional hobby, an accessory to a life of comfort. In a culture engineered for mental drift, the disciplined choice to learn is the highest form of self-authorship. It is a refusal to be shaped by the crowd.

And to be clear: when I use the word "identity," I'm not referring to the cultural or political meaning often used today. I'm speaking of identity in the older, deeper sense—your God-given design, your purpose, your orientation toward truth, and the internal alignment with the person you were created to become.

Learning isn't a technique. It's a posture toward the world.

It's how you decide who you will become.

And in a culture that has quietly abandoned it, learning becomes a rare and powerful advantage.

Identity Before Information

We live in a time when information is everywhere, yet wisdom is scarce. People consume endlessly—swiping, scrolling, reacting—but they almost never wrestle with an idea long enough to let it shape who they are. Learning has been replaced by entertainment; reflection by stimulation. Modern life makes it easy to stay mentally full and spiritually empty. This is the tangible cost of not learning: your fragmented attention ensures that you not only miss new ideas, but you fail to execute the ones you already have. You suffer from a poverty of application, not information.

The ancient thinkers understood this deeply. Marcus Aurelius wrote, "The soul becomes dyed with the color of its thoughts." This was a warning, not poetry: What you take in becomes who you are. Attention is not neutral. Every input paints a stroke on the character you're becoming. Neuroscience confirms what the Stoics intuited: the mind rewires itself continuously based on focus. Your identity forms around your inputs. When those inputs are shallow or passive, the resulting identity is as thin as the information that shaped it. When learning is central—intentional, disciplined, and reflective—identity becomes strong, steady, and directed.

The Fifth-Grade Moment That Changed Everything

My commitment to learning began earlier than I understood. In the fifth grade, my dad offered me five dollars to read Zig Ziglar's See You at the Top. That small deal became the first intentional block of my self-made foundation. Ziglar's clarity and optimism were a compass that pierced the noise of childhood. He taught me that mindset is not an accessory; it is the ultimate discipline. A person rises or falls based on the thoughts they choose, and the most fulfilled people are the ones who help others rise.

Later in life, Ziglar's famous line became one of my all-time favorite principles:

"You can have everything in life you want if you will just help enough other people get what they want."

That idea didn't just influence how I saw success; it shaped how I saw purpose.

Another image from Ziglar's book stayed with me as well: his contrast between heaven and hell. Two banquet tables. Long-handled spoons strapped to people's arms. In hell, everyone starves because they try to feed themselves. In heaven, everyone thrives because they feed one another. That picture etched something into me at a young age — that growth, purpose, and learning are ultimately about service.

From that fifth-grade moment on, I saw the world differently. I became an optimist. Not naïve — resolved. Learning was no longer just about information. It was about becoming the kind of person who could contribute, serve, and lead.

Becoming the Person You Were Created to Be

Years later, Matthew Kelly's writings helped frame what I had felt since childhood: learning isn't about achievement — it's about becoming the best version of yourself. Growth is a sacred responsibility. It honors God's design and equips you to serve the world more effectively.

That perspective strengthened something I already believed intuitively: learning is spiritual before it is practical.

It is obedience to potential.

It is stewardship of the gift of your life.

And when you treat learning as identity, everything changes:

You choose better inputs.

You pursue deeper thinking.

You take responsibility for who you are becoming.

You recognize that character is formed — not found.

Learning becomes the engine of purpose.

Why Learning Is a Competitive Advantage

We live in a paradox. Information has never been more abundant, yet true learners have never been more rare. Most people aren't thinking — they're reacting. They aren't reading — they're consuming. They aren't growing — they're drifting.

This is why learning gives you an edge.

Not because you're smarter.

Not because you're exceptional.

But because you are willing to do what most people no longer consider.

When attention is fragmented, the one who can focus advances.

When comfort is king, the one who chooses discipline matures.

When everyone is overstimulated, the one who thinks clearly becomes invaluable.

Learning creates separation — not for superiority, but for stewardship. When you learn deeply, you become more capable, more grounded, and more useful to your family, your work, and your community.

The younger generation, especially, has an unprecedented opportunity. While many struggle with distraction and drift, a young person who takes learning seriously will outpace their peers in every area of life. Not because they have more potential, but because they choose to cultivate it.

Learning as Calling

At its core, learning is not about accumulation. It is about preparation. It's how you build the character, discipline, clarity, and humility required to live out your calling.

If you abandon learning, you slowly abandon purpose. You stop seeing clearly. You stop growing meaningfully. Drift sets in — quietly, gradually, predictably.

But when learning is part of who you are, you stay aligned. You stay sharp. You stay connected to the deeper currents of meaning running beneath the surface of daily life.

Learning is how you become who you must be in order to do what you were created to do.

The Foundation for Everything That Comes Next

This book is built on a simple truth:

Learning shapes identity, and identity shapes destiny.

Everything that follows — comfort addiction, overstimulation, dopamine, discipline, paradigm control, vocation, humility, gratitude, systems, habits, and even AI — is built on this first principle. If learning is not part of your identity, the rest of the tools won't matter.

But if it is, everything becomes possible.

Recommended Book

See You at the Top — Zig Ziglar
A classic on personal identity, character, and mental conditioning. Ziglar argues that who you become is the foundation of everything you do.

Comfort Is an Addiction

CHAPTER 2

"It is not that life is hard,
but that we make it so by craving ease."

— Seneca

omfort is appealing because it feels natural. But the truth is the opposite: comfort rarely aligns with how we were made. Human beings were created for exertion, responsibility, and purposeful struggle. The human body was engineered for survival; the modern couch was engineered for immediate, irreversible surrender. The first task given to a human being was work, not leisure. Formation has always been tied to effort. Identity has always been shaped under pressure. Purpose has always been revealed through responsibility. When comfort becomes a priority, a person begins living in a way that contradicts their design.

Most people don't recognize this. Comfort feels good. It promises simplicity and relief. But it quietly removes the very conditions that build a strong, capable, meaningful life. Ease doesn't strengthen character; it erodes it. It interrupts the process of becoming. It cuts a person off from the friction that shapes identity and sharpens clarity.

The esteemed Roman emperor and Stoic philosopher, Marcus Aurelius, once observed that the craving for ease is "man's greatest addiction."

This insight captures a timeless truth now manifesting in the modern world. As we become increasingly enveloped in comfort and convenience—from climate-controlled homes to instant access to everything—we risk losing the very resilience and growth that come from facing life's inherent challenges.

I've experienced this personally. I went through a period where I drifted toward ease — not out of rebellion, but out of subtle neglect. I stepped away from challenge because slowing down felt justified. The longer I stayed in that place, the more disoriented I became. What I thought would simplify my life ended up weakening it. I lost the sharpness that comes from responsibility and the sense of direction that comes from carrying weight. That season taught me that comfort is not neutral; it pushes you away from formation.

The Physiological Cost of Convenience

Neuroscience confirms this pattern. Andrew Huberman's work shows that the human brain requires stress, challenge, and resistance to function correctly. When life becomes consistently easy, the nervous system adapts downward. Motivation decreases, energy declines, and ambition fades. The mind is not designed for endless comfort; it is designed to grow through effort.

Physicians like Dr. Jason Fung highlight a related metabolic crisis: the comfort of modern diets and continuous food availability deprives our bodies of the natural metabolic flexibility that comes from periods of fasting or scarcity. Our bodies, evolved for cycles of feast and famine, are now constantly flooded, leading to metabolic fragility. Similarly, Wim Hof, known as "The Iceman," argues that our over-reliance on comfort— heated rooms and soft environments has disconnected us from the natural stimuli (like cold) essential for optimal biological functioning. By insulating ourselves from these natural stressors, we dull our innate physical and mental resilience.

One of the most eye-opening demonstrations of how the body responds to deliberate discomfort is something I've walked well over a hundred people through: Wim Hof's breathing technique. It's one of the rare practices where you can *feel* your physiology shift in real time. You don't need technology, labs, or gadgets — just your breath and a timer. And what it shows is simple: most people have never actually tested the systems built into them.

The method itself mimics a controlled version of hyperventilation. That sounds intense, but it is simply a way to momentarily stress the body so you can observe its natural defenses activating. The exercise begins with a baseline breath-hold. Take a deep breath in, let it out naturally, and start your timer. Hold until you must inhale again. Most adults land somewhere between twenty-five seconds and a minute. That number doesn't measure strength or fitness — it measures unfamiliarity with this system.

Then comes the part that reveals what modern comfort hides. Reset, sit down safely, and take thirty full, aggressive breaths: all the way in, all the way out, fast. By the twenties, people usually feel a wave of dizziness and tingling in their fingers. That's not danger; it's physiology responding to a sudden shift in oxygen and carbon dioxide levels. If someone doesn't feel anything at all, their pace is usually off. The goal is to fully load the system and unload it just as quickly — a controlled stressor that almost no one experiences in normal life.

On breath thirty (or thirty-one — it doesn't matter), take one last deep inhale, let the air out, and immediately start your second timer. Same process: hold as long as you can, letting air out if you need to, but the moment you inhale again, the round ends.

This is where eyes widen. Nearly everyone doubles their time. Someone who held for forty seconds on round one suddenly lasts a minute and a half. Someone who started at a minute often reaches two minutes. I've seen people who naturally hold their breath for two minutes hit three minutes on the first attempt. Not because they became superhuman in sixty seconds — but because they activated a system they've never accessed before.

That change isn't magic. It's biology. Research on Hof's method shows several key benefits that explain what people feel during the exercise:

- **Increased carbon dioxide tolerance**
  CO_2 tolerance improves instantly, making breath-holds dramatically easier.

- **Greater oxygen efficiency**
  The body becomes more effective at distributing and using oxygen under stress.

- **Activation of the parasympathetic nervous system**
  After the breathing cycle, the nervous system shifts into a calm, regulated state.

- **Temporary adrenaline surge**
  A controlled spike that sharpens awareness and primes the system.

- **Reduced inflammatory response**
  Multiple studies show lower inflammatory markers in people who practice the method consistently.

- **Heightened stress resilience**
  The exercise trains the body to stay functional under discomfort.

In other words, the technique reveals the machinery comfort hides. For most people, life is so easy and climate-controlled that their stress-response mechanisms rarely turn on. Wim Hof's breathing cycle wakes them up. The dizziness, the tingling, the breath-hold jump — these sensations are your body proving that it is capable of responding, adapting, and protecting you when challenged.

The technique is uncomfortable by design. But that discomfort provides a glimpse into a deeper truth: the body is far more capable than the lifestyle we've built around it. When you briefly reintroduce discomfort — even in something as simple as structured breathing — you activate systems you were always meant to use. You feel capacity where you assumed limitation. You see firsthand that fragility isn't your nature; it's your conditioning.

And that's why this fits perfectly in a chapter about comfort as addiction. Comfort dulls the systems meant to strengthen us. Discomfort awakens them. This little breathing experiment is not about breath-holding — it's about rediscovering what's built into you when you stop insulating yourself from challenge. It is a moment of biological clarity: the limits you feel aren't your actual limits, they're just the result of a life without friction.

This is why ancient traditions — Stoic, monastic, and biblical — always treated effort as a necessary part of becoming fully human. The Stoics, whose wisdom is explored in depth by modern interpreters like Ryan Holiday (who argues that The Obstacle Is the Way), practiced deliberate hardship to stay aligned with reality, knowing that challenges require the disciplined response of perception, action, and will. Monastic communities embraced disciplines that developed endurance, clarity, and interior strength. Scripture and tradition consistently tie growth to perseverance, not avoidance. These aren't random historical quirks. They reflect something fundamental about humanity: we grow through tension, not escape.

C.S. Lewis captured this idea when he wrote that chasing comfort directly produces neither truth nor comfort. A person ends up restless, dissatisfied, and spiritually heavy because they've stepped outside the pattern their soul is meant to live in. Comfort feels good in the moment, but it distorts everything in the long run — purpose, identity, and even one's sense of self.

When comfort becomes the default, you see a predictable decline. A person begins to expect ease. They begin to interpret difficulty as injustice rather than formation. Responsibility feels like a burden rather than a calling. Their world becomes smaller because they avoid the very things that would expand it. And slowly, the identity that once felt strong becomes fragile.

This is one of the greatest issues facing younger generations today. They are surrounded by convenience and overstimulation that eliminates almost all natural friction. They are told that discomfort is a problem, challenge is trauma, and difficulty is a sign that something is wrong. But every generation before them understood the opposite: effort is how you grow. Pain is how you learn. The challenge is how you become someone capable of carrying meaning.

The opportunity here is enormous. When everyone around you is shaped by comfort, the person who accepts challenge gains immediate separation. Not because they are more talented or fortunate, but because they are living closer to the design written into human nature.

Comfort is not the enemy because it's sinful. Comfort is the enemy because it's disordered. It places a person in opposition to the grain of their own humanity. It removes the struggle that forges strength. It blocks the tension that sharpens discernment. It cuts off the friction that reveals purpose. And the result is always the same: drift, confusion, and a shrinking sense of self.

Discomfort isn't noble in itself — it's necessary. It is the natural environment where clarity emerges, and identity solidifies. It is the context where discipline becomes possible and where purpose becomes visible. To reject discomfort is to reject the process of becoming. Pick your difficulty: the hard work of discipline or the hard work of perpetual cleanup. And to embrace comfort as a way of life is to quietly surrender your growth.

The human soul knows this, whether we acknowledge it or not. A life built on ease never feels right for long. It leaves a hollow ache because the soul senses it is not being formed. But once a person engages with a challenge — intellectual, spiritual, or physical — something awakens. The mind sharpens. The heart steadies. Purpose becomes clearer. The person remembers who they are capable of becoming.

The truth is simple: comfort feels natural only because it is immediately pleasant. It is not natural in the deeper sense of aligning with who we were made to be. Human beings are wired for growth, not stagnation.

For responsibility, not withdrawal. For effort, not escape. And when you align your life with that design, everything changes: purpose expands, identity strengthens, and learning becomes a way of life.

This sets the foundation for understanding discomfort not as an obstacle to avoid, but as the environment where a meaningful life actually takes shape.

Recommended Book

The Comfort Crisis: Embrace Discomfort to Reclaim Your Wild, Happy, Healthy Self — Michael Easter
A research-driven look at why modern ease weakens resilience and how deliberately embracing discomfort restores strength, clarity, and alignment with how humans were designed to grow.

Overstimulation, Noise, and Attention Theft

"All of humanity's problems stem from man's inability to sit quietly in a room alone."

— Blaise Pascal

Human beings were designed for depth, for contemplation, and for meaningful attention. Our nature was built around the ability to focus, reflect, and engage intentionally with the world around us. But we live in the most overstimulated era in human history — an environment that chips away at the very structure of attention itself.

When distraction becomes normal, depth feels foreign.

And when depth feels foreign, meaning becomes hard to access.

Picking up from the previous chapter: if identity is shaped through learning and comfort weakens the will, then overstimulation fractures the very tool that makes learning — and ultimately identity — possible: attention.

We don't just live with noise; we inhale it.

The modern world is engineered to steal attention at scale. My phone is the least productive slot machine I have ever played, and yet I keep pulling the lever. The only jackpot is ten minutes of mental clarity, and I've already blown that on the walk over. As observers like Tristan Harris of the Center for Humane Technology point out, this is not an accident—it is an economic model. Apps, feeds, alerts, pings, streams, and algorithms compete for the same resource: your mind's ability to direct itself. Human attention has become a commodity; companies fight for it, technology reshapes it, and distraction profits from it. And the more fractured it becomes, the more incapable a person is of living with clarity or purpose.

I've felt that pull myself. Even with years of discipline, leadership, and spiritual formation behind me, I still feel the gravitational tug toward mindless entertainment and scrolling. It's embarrassingly easy to slip into. What starts as a quick check becomes fragmented minutes, then fragmented thoughts. You don't notice it immediately, but eventually, you realize your mind is buzzing, restless, and unable to land. It reinforces what Pascal observed centuries ago: sitting quietly—without stimulation—feels almost impossible because our minds have been rewired to resist stillness.

Overstimulation doesn't just distract us. It reshapes us.

Cal Newport identifies this reality clearly: "Focus is the new IQ in the modern economy." He's right, but not simply because deep work is productive. Focus is the new IQ because most people can no longer sustain it. Their attention has been fractured by the constant drip of digital noise. The ability to think deeply has become so rare that those who cultivate it gain an immediate advantage—not because they're smarter, but because they're less distracted.

The difference between the distracted mind and the focused mind is the difference between a floodlight and a laser. The floodlight illuminates a wide area but has no power, unable to cut through resistance or create heat. The laser concentrates its energy onto a single point, allowing it to cut through difficulty and heat up an idea until it yields wisdom.

The modern flood of stimulation is more than an inconvenience; it's a threat to identity. Identity is formed through reflection, not reaction. Through conscious choice, not constant interruption. Through the ability to sit with thoughts long enough to understand what they mean. Attention is the physical manifestation of free will. If you can't choose what to focus on, you lose the ability to choose who you are. When distraction becomes constant, the mind becomes a place where thoughts pass through but never take shape.

This is why overstimulation feels like friction: it competes with the part of you designed to seek meaning.

Theological traditions have always emphasized the importance of guarding attention. Silence wasn't valued because noise was bad; silence was valued because attention is sacred. Scripture repeatedly presents focus as a path to wisdom — "Be still and know…" is not poetic filler; it's spiritual architecture. Stillness is where a person regains alignment. But overstimulation makes stillness feel like deprivation.

And that's the heart of the problem: overstimulation creates an internal climate where stillness feels uncomfortable, reflection feels unnatural, and depth feels inaccessible. The mind becomes accustomed to shallow engagement — quick, easy hits of stimulation rather than the slower, deliberate pace of wisdom.

Yet the person who learns to think deeply gains clarity in a world of noise.

The person who learns to resist overstimulation gains strength where others lose it.

And the person who guards attention becomes someone capable of intentional growth.

Overstimulation isn't just the enemy of productivity; it's the enemy of formation. When attention is fractured, comfort becomes more appealing, challenge becomes more difficult, and learning becomes less possible. This chapter establishes the final part of the triad begun in the book's opening: Identity requires learning, learning requires discomfort, and discomfort requires focused attention.

Without attention, nothing meaningful grows.

Every profound accomplishment — whether spiritual, intellectual, relational, or professional — requires extended periods of focus. Every major transformation in a person's life happens when they direct their mind toward something specific long enough for it to matter. But the modern world makes that nearly impossible unless you deliberately resist it.

The good news is that attention can be rebuilt. The mind adapts. It strengthens. It remembers depth when you return to it. And because so few people are doing this work, the smallest gains matter. Fifteen minutes of focused reading today separates you from half the population. Thirty minutes of uninterrupted thought separates you from even more. Not because the culture is unintelligent, but because it is overstimulated.

When you learn to push back against noise — when you learn to take your attention seriously — you become someone capable of clarity in a world that has lost it. You begin to see opportunities others miss. You begin to hear ideas others overlook. You begin to feel a sense of direction that cuts through the chaos. By guarding your attention, you are practicing a daily form of moral and mental discipline—a commitment to a chosen identity over a manufactured one.

Overstimulation steals attention.

Attention shapes identity.

Therefore, overstimulation steals identity.

The path back is not dramatic or complicated. It begins with the simple acknowledgment that attention is worth fighting for. That your mind is worth protecting. That noise does not deserve the authority it has been given. And that a focused life is not only possible but necessary if you want to live in alignment with the person God designed you to become.

Recommended Books

Indistractable: How to Control Your Attention and Choose Your Life — Nir Eyal
A behavioral framework for understanding how distraction hijacks your mind and how reclaiming attention is the gateway to clarity and intentional living.

Deep Work: Rules for Focused Success in a Distracted World — Cal Newport
A foundational text on the power of sustained concentration, explaining why deep focus is the new competitive advantage in a noisy, overstimulated world.

Dopamine Detoxing and the Resetting of Motivation

CHAPTER 4

"Too much pleasure is pain."

— Blaise Pascal

Modern life is overstimulated to the point of distortion. The mind was not designed for constant novelty, endless entertainment, or the frictionless stream of micro-rewards that digital life provides. Yet this is the environment nearly everyone lives in — a world where dopamine spikes all day long, almost always from low-effort, low-value distractions.

This creates a neurological problem that becomes a spiritual problem, then a motivational problem, then an identity problem. When dopamine is constantly activated, the brain's reward system dulls. Pleasure loses impact. Curiosity fades. Motivation collapses. The person feels restless, bored, unmotivated, and vaguely dissatisfied — without understanding why.

This is the territory where dopamine detoxing enters — not as a trend or a hack, but as a scientific reset of the mind's motivational circuitry.

The Physiology of a Fried Reward System

Dopamine is often misunderstood as the molecule of pleasure. In reality, it's the molecule of pursuit — of anticipation, of drive, of wanting. Modern overstimulation hijacks that system by offering dopamine spikes without requiring meaningful effort. The brain adapts downward, meaning it takes more stimulation to get the same response, and the baseline of motivation drops.

The neuroscientist Dr. Anna Lembke, a leading expert on addiction, clarifies this through the concept of the pleasure-pain balance. Every time we chase an intense, low-effort hit of dopamine—from a social media alert, a sugar rush, or a moment of digital consumption—the brain counterbalances that pleasure with a corresponding shift toward pain. When we repeatedly engage in this behavior, the brain's "set point" permanently shifts, leaving us with a chronic, low-level state of deficit, often experienced as anxiety, restlessness, or anhedonia (the inability to feel joy from normal activities).

This is why overstimulated people often feel:

- mentally foggy

- easily distracted

- unable to finish tasks

- burned out

- bored even with things they love

- trapped in cycles of mindless consumption

The problem isn't willpower.

The problem is neurobiology. You know you're dopamine-fried when folding your laundry feels like running a marathon, but watching five hours of a documentary series you hate feels like 'unwinding.' The scale is broken.

Cal Newport explains this indirectly through his work on focus — deep concentration requires a mind that hasn't been overstimulated into fragmentation. Thibaut Meurisse puts it plainly in his writing on dopamine detoxing: if you gorge your brain on quick hits, you destroy your hunger for meaningful work.

This is not moral weakness. It is biological adaptation.

The Loss of Motivation

When dopamine pathways are saturated, ambition feels inaccessible. The motivation to do deep work, pursue goals, learn, think, or push through difficulty fades beneath the constant desire for something easier and more instantly rewarding.

The tragedy is that the person often blames themselves. They assume something is wrong with their discipline, their mindset, or their identity. But the issue sits upstream: a reward system overloaded with noise.

A dopamine-fried mind doesn't want to work toward meaningful goals — it wants escape. It wants stimulation. It wants the next hit of novelty because it has forgotten how to enjoy anything deeper.

This explains why so many people today feel stuck despite having more opportunities, information, and tools than any generation before them. They are not lazy — they are overstimulated. An overstimulated mind cannot pursue meaning.

Spiritual and Philosophical Parallels

The church fathers, Stoics, monks, and ancient teachers all wrote about forms of restraint that sound almost identical to modern dopamine research — not because they understood neurochemistry, but because they understood human nature.

The monastic traditions practiced seasons of input reduction to sharpen attention and restore clarity. Stoics warned about the dangers of constant indulgence because they knew it weakened the soul's resilience. In spiritual language, the more you feed your desires, the more they govern you. In scientific language, the more you overstimulate dopamine, the less responsive the system becomes.

These two worlds — ancient and modern — describe the same human pattern from different angles:

When you constantly chase stimulation, you lose the ability to pursue purpose.

The Reset

A dopamine detox is not deprivation. It is alignment.

It is the deliberate reduction of hyper-stimulating inputs so the reward system can recalibrate.

When the baseline resets:

- Ambition returns

- Focus becomes possible

- Curiosity resurfaces

- Deep work feels satisfying

- Boredom becomes a doorway to clarity rather than something to escape.

This is the competitive advantage hidden in the modern crisis. While most people continue numbing themselves with endless stimulation, a person who reduces inputs — even slightly — regains a level of motivation and drive that others barely remember.

This is why learning becomes easier after a detox. The mind becomes hungry again. Ideas feel interesting. The desire to build, create, read, and grow resurfaces. The reset restores the natural cycle of effort → reward → satisfaction that overstimulation breaks.

The Identity Implication

A person's sense of self degrades when dopamine is overloaded. They feel scattered, unfocused, restless, and inconsistent. They struggle to follow through because the mind refuses to engage with anything that requires sustained effort. This leads to self-doubt and internal friction.

But when the dopamine system resets, confidence returns — not because the person became stronger, but because they regained access to their natural drive.

When the mind is quiet, identity becomes clearer.

When motivation is restored, discipline becomes possible.

When discipline becomes possible, learning becomes identity again.

We need to restore the engine of that identity: the capacity to want deeply, to pursue meaningfully, and to grow consistently.

Dopamine detoxing is not about giving something up. It is about reclaiming the part of you that modern life has overloaded: desire itself.

For readers who want a practical, walk-through version of the dopamine reset process, I've created a free companion guide available at **https://abl.codetap.ai**. It expands on the ideas in this chapter and provides a clear, actionable framework you can begin using immediately.

Recommended Books

Dopamine Detox — Thibaut Meurisse
A clear and practical breakdown of how overstimulation erodes motivation and how resetting the dopamine system reignites the desire for meaningful work.

Dopamine Nation: Finding Balance in the Age of Indulgence — Anna Lembke
A scientific and compelling examination of how constant pleasure-

seeking rewires the brain toward pain—and why intentional discomfort is essential for contentment.

PART

II

THE INTERNAL FOUNDATION

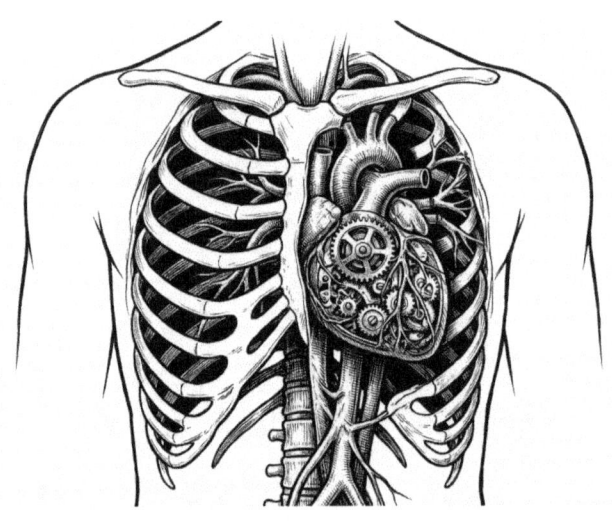

Once the external world is understood, the real battle begins inside. Part II explores the identity, virtues, and inner architecture that make lifelong learning possible. Learning is not primarily a technique — it is a way of seeing the world and a way of seeing yourself.

Identity anchors intention. Purpose provides direction. Paradigms shape interpretation. Gratitude steadies the mind. Humility protects the learner from fragility and arrogance. These virtues form the internal scaffolding that carries a person through decades of growth.

This section draws deeply from your manuscript's central convictions: growth is a sacred obligation, learning is an act of humility, and meaning is found through alignment with calling. When a person knows who they are and what they are becoming, learning becomes natural, sustainable, and joyful.

This section builds the learner from the inside out. It gives the reader the worldview required to grow for a lifetime — not with strain, but with purpose, identity, and theological grounding.

CHAPTER 5

The Discipline
To Do Hard Things

*"If you always choose the easy path,
you never become who you're supposed to be."*

— David Goggins

Human beings were created with the capacity to endure, persevere, and grow stronger through difficulty. This isn't a motivational idea; it's embedded into the structure of our nature. The body strengthens under resistance. The mind sharpens under challenge. The soul matures when it shoulders responsibility. Discipline is not a punishment — it is the operating system that unlocks human potential.

Modern life makes effort look optional, almost unnecessary. Convenience is everywhere. Hardship is framed as a problem to escape. Technology promises shortcuts for everything, making difficulty feel outdated or inefficient. But whenever ease becomes the default, the muscles of character begin to atrophy — slowly, quietly, predictably.

Goggins captures this reality with blunt clarity. Hard things don't just build toughness; they reveal identity. The willingness to embrace difficulty separates those who drift from those who grow. Choosing the easy path doesn't mean you avoid hard things. It just means the hard things you face are now debt, poor health, and regret. It's not about masochism or self-punishment. It's about confronting the resistance that shapes a person from the inside out. Most people avoid that resistance. The few who lean into it — physically, intellectually, spiritually — tap into capacities they never knew they had.

This philosophy long predates the modern world. Marcus Aurelius wrote that obstacles are not interruptions to progress, but the very material progress is made. Hardship doesn't block the path; it is the path. To refuse a difficult task is to refuse the opportunity to become someone capable. To accept it is to participate in your own development.

The Neuroscience of Voluntarily Chosen Effort

This ancient wisdom is now confirmed by modern science. The core of discipline lies in strengthening the Prefrontal Cortex (PFC), the brain's executive control center responsible for long-term planning, decision-making, and delayed gratification. When you consciously override the desire for immediate comfort (the emotional brain) to choose a harder, more purposeful action (the rational brain), you are literally training the PFC. Each act of voluntary, non-immediate effort is a repetition that builds mental endurance. Discipline, in this sense, is simply the practice of making your future self's best interests a reality today. This is why a person who does hard things in one area of life often sees their focus and commitment improve everywhere else—the neural pathway for choosing the difficult over the easy becomes stronger.

The ancient world understood something we've largely forgotten: you cannot separate growth from strain. Discipline takes the theoretical and forces it into the real. It pushes ideals into practice. It grounds intention in action. It transforms a person not by what they believe, but by what they are willing to endure.

Even in spiritual traditions, discipline is not treated as an accessory but as a foundation. St. Francis lived with radical intentionality, embracing simplicity and sacrifice not to prove anything, but to align himself with what mattered most. His life demonstrated a truth echoed across centuries: discipline purifies desire. When you willingly choose the harder road, you begin to see your motives, your strengths, and your weaknesses with sharper clarity. You discover what is real.

This alignment between ancient philosophy, modern psychology, and spiritual wisdom points to a universal reality: human beings are at their best when they consistently engage with difficult things. Discipline is the instrument through which intention becomes identity. Without it, potential remains theoretical. With it, potential becomes tangible.

In practical terms, doing hard things recalibrates how you see yourself. When you voluntarily take on difficult tasks — whether physical challenges, demanding work, rigorous study, or acts of service — you break the internal narrative that comfort is the safer choice. Difficulty becomes less threatening and more familiar. You start to trust yourself. You know you can rely on your own will. That confidence carries into every area of life.

Difficulty also clarifies priorities. When something is hard, you have to decide whether it matters. Hard tasks strip away distraction and force focus. They reveal commitment. They make you choose who you want to be, not who you feel like being in the moment. Discipline forms identity by confronting you with that choice repeatedly.

This is why discipline is transformative even before it produces results. The act of pushing through friction — regardless of the outcome — creates internal alignment. Hard things awaken agency. They renew purpose. They reconnect you to the structural strength built into the human person.

Most people today avoid difficulty instinctively, not knowing they are avoiding the very process that would make their lives meaningful. They want clarity without pressure, confidence without challenge, competence without repetition, and purpose without sacrifice. But life doesn't work that way. The things worth having require effort, and the person worthy of stewarding them is forged through that effort.

When you choose to do hard things, you reintroduce yourself to what you are capable of. You begin to see difficulty not as an obstacle, but as a teacher. You start recognizing the quiet opportunities embedded in tasks others run from. You feel the internal shift from passive living to active formation.

And in a world where convenience has become the default lifestyle, the capacity to embrace difficulty becomes a rare and powerful advantage. Most people will continue seeking shortcuts. Most will retreat from resistance. Most will treat discomfort as a threat. Those who choose the harder path — deliberately, repeatedly, and without theatrics — will grow while others stagnate.

Discipline doesn't just strengthen you. It distinguishes you.

It turns effort into identity.

It transforms difficulty into direction.

It grounds purpose in action.

Doing hard things is not about proving anything to others. It's about refusing to live beneath your design. It's about becoming the kind of person capable of carrying responsibility, creating value, and living a meaningful life. It's about aligning your daily choices with the deeper truth of who you are meant to become.

Discipline is the doorway. Difficulty is the curriculum. Growth is the outcome.

Recommended Book

Can't Hurt Me — David Goggins
A raw, unfiltered look at the power of embracing difficulty. Goggins shows how mental toughness is built through deliberate confrontation with resistance, revealing how identity is forged under strain.

CHAPTER 6

Framing Purpose:
Work, Worship & Service

"Work is not what you do.
It's part of who you are becoming."

— Matthew Kelly

Purpose is not a luxury. It is a requirement baked into the structure of human nature. Just as the body needs food and the mind needs challenge, the soul needs meaning to function correctly. A life lived without a clear sense of why is a life defined by drift—easily seduced by comfort, easily fractured by distraction, and easily defeated by difficulty. The central task of the learner is not to find a job or a hobby but to organize their life around a vocation that aligns their daily actions with their deepest convictions.

Viktor Frankl and the Will to Meaning

The twentieth-century psychiatrist Viktor Frankl, a Holocaust survivor, observed that the ultimate human motivation is the "will to meaning," a profound drive to find purpose in existence. Frankl's work led him to develop Logotherapy, the principle that even in the most horrific circumstances, a person can choose their response and find meaning, often through work, love, or courage in the face of suffering. The most tragic condition, he argued, is not suffering itself, but meaningless suffering.

This is the philosophical counterpoint to the Modern Condition: when you live in a world of comfort and distraction, the pain is low, but the meaning is also low. Purpose is not about minimizing friction; it is about maximizing the value of the friction you encounter. The learner understands that meaningful work is what protects the self from spiritual collapse.

The Three Pillars of Vocation

To frame a meaningful life—a life of intentional, disciplined learning—we must align all energy toward three integrated pillars that form a complete vocation: Work, Worship, and Service.

1. Work (The Pillar of Creation): This is the application of your gifts, energy, and learned skills to create value in the world. It may be your professional career, a side project, or the management of your home and family. Work is the mechanism by which your learning is tested in the crucible of reality. It requires discipline, focus, and competence.

2. Worship (The Pillar of Perspective): This is the deliberate practice of centering yourself on something greater than your own life, ambition, or feelings. It provides the essential perspective that your life is not ultimate, anchoring your identity and protecting you from the ego-driven trap of making your career an idol. It reminds you of the source of your gifts and the object of your obedience.

3. Service (The Pillar of Alignment): This is the act of directing your created value and your centered perspective outwardly to help other people. It is the core of Zig Ziglar's wisdom and the final test of all learning. Service ensures that personal ambition does not become hoarding and that growth is never for superiority, but for stewardship.

The danger is not in doing one of these things, but in separating them. I have personally wrestled with seasons where I over-indexed on Work, chasing success and achievement to the detriment of Service and

Worship. The result was not fulfillment but burnout and a quiet sense of spiritual emptiness. The work was productive, but it lacked meaning. It only restored my purpose when I intentionally re-anchored my daily decisions to the realization that my energy was a resource meant to be deployed for a calling larger than myself.

The Example of George Washington Carver

For a powerful demonstration of this alignment, consider the life of scientist George Washington Carver. Carver, an agricultural chemist, could have easily leveraged his genius for immense personal wealth, but he famously dedicated his life and work to the poor, struggling farmers of the South. His research—including over 300 uses for the peanut and hundreds more for sweet potatoes—was a radical act of service to a community in desperate need. For Carver, his laboratory was not just a workplace; it was an altar. His learning was not for personal acclaim; it was a way of honoring his faith and serving his neighbors. He synthesized the three pillars: his work was his inventive genius, his Worship was his guiding faith, and his Service was the donation of his entire life's intellectual property to solve other people's problems. His purpose was unbreakable because its roots were anchored in contribution, not comfort.

Purpose is found not at the intersection of your passions, but at the intersection of these three pillars. When they are aligned, learning feels essential because it is fueling your vocation. When they are unaligned, learning feels optional because it serves no greater end than temporary personal gain.

The ultimate goal of the disciplined learner is to build a life where their work is a form of their worship, and their worship inevitably leads them to service. This is the inner structure required to sustain growth for a lifetime.

Recommended Book

Resisting Happiness—Matthew Kelly
A practical and spiritual exploration of the internal resistance that keeps people from living with purpose, clarity, and intentionality. Kelly reveals why people settle, why they avoid the disciplines that would transform their lives, and how choosing meaning over comfort is the first step toward a life of direction.

Paradigm Mastery: The Mental Tool That Changes Everything

"What you see and what you hear depends a great deal on where you are standing."

— C.S. Lewis

Human beings do not respond to life; they respond to their interpretation of life. This interpretation—the lens through which you see reality—is called a paradigm. It is the non-negotiable mental operating system that dictates how you process information, interpret motives, define success, and ultimately, decide who you are.

The problem is that most people operate on unexamined, inherited, or outdated paradigms. They live under a mental map that was drawn by their culture, their family history, or their past failures. They apply great discipline to a flawed map, leading to immense effort and predictable frustration. This is why the disciplined learner must first become a Paradigm Master: the ability to choose your own map is the ultimate mental tool.

The Map, Not the Territory

The late Stephen Covey, whose work is built on the power of paradigms, famously stated that the map is not the territory. Your paradigm is the map you carry—a collection of assumptions, beliefs, and values. A paradigm is a mental map. If you're using a map from 1998, you can have all the discipline in the world; you're still going to end up confused in a Blockbuster Video parking lot. Update your map. The territory is reality itself. If your map is wrong, your will and effort are irrelevant. If the map of marriage tells you that conflict is failure, you will sabotage your relationship. If your map of business tells you that success is purely a factor of luck, you will stop trying.

The most fundamental shift in becoming a learner is the conscious realization that when there is a conflict between your view of the world and the results you get from the world, the error is always in the map. The solution is not to try harder but to change the map.

The Anatomy of a Paradigm Shift

This power of perspective is not just a personal tool; it is the engine of all human progress. The philosopher of science Thomas Kuhn introduced the concept of the "paradigm shift" in his influential book, The Structure of Scientific Revolutions. Kuhn argued that major scientific breakthroughs—from Galileo's heliocentric model to Einstein's theory of relativity—do not occur by simply collecting new facts. They occur when the entire scientific community abandons an old paradigm (a stable framework for understanding the world) and replaces it with a fundamentally new one.

In personal terms, a paradigm shift is not a gradual change. It is an abrupt, total reorientation of how you see your capability, your purpose, or your history.

- A business owner shifts from a Scarcity Paradigm (I must hoard resources) to an Abundance Paradigm (I must create value).

- A person in recovery shifts from an Addiction Paradigm (I am a failure) to a Growth Paradigm (I am a student of my weakness).

- The disciplined learner shifts from a Fixed Paradigm (My intelligence is static) to a Mastery Paradigm (My intelligence is a result of my deliberate effort).

This is the moment of greatest leverage. By replacing the core operating system of your mind, you make discipline easier, discomfort clearer, and learning inevitable. The most crucial work of a learner is to constantly challenge, test, and rewrite the mental maps they inherited.

The Three Disciplines of Paradigm Mastery

Paradigm Mastery is not passive contemplation; it is an active discipline of intentional learning and application:

1. Seek the Anomaly: Actively look for data points that contradict your current beliefs. The mark of a rigid mind is to dismiss inconvenient facts. The mark of a learner is to aggressively seek out the knowledge that threatens their existing paradigm.

2. Own the Map: Take complete responsibility for your current mental model. If your current paradigm is causing emotional, relational, or professional failure, do not blame the territory (reality); accept that the flaw is in the map you are using.

3. Model the New Reality: Once you identify a flawed paradigm, consciously adopt a new one by consuming the inputs that shape it. If you want a Growth Paradigm, you must exclusively read, listen to, and surround yourself with people who operate from that place. You must be willing to let the old you die for the new you to live.

Mastery is impossible without this foundational work. A learner cannot live out a profound purpose while clinging to a shallow or fearful map. Discipline is merely the fuel. Paradigm Mastery is the ignition that points fuel in the right direction. It ensures that the power of your efforts is aligned with the deepest truths of reality.

Recommended Book

The 7 Habits of Highly Effective People: Powerful Lessons in Personal Change — Stephen R. Covey

A foundational work on paradigm shifts, personal responsibility, and character-based growth. Covey's approach provides the practical framework for transforming your mental maps and aligning behavior with principle-driven effectiveness.

CHAPTER 8

Gratitude:
A Well-Known Superpower

"I would maintain that thanks
are the highest form of thought."

— G.K. Chesterton

Gratitude is one of the most misunderstood forces in the human experience. People treat it as a soft virtue, a pleasant idea, a moral nicety. But gratitude is far more than an emotion—it is a cognitive superpower. It rewires perception, stabilizes the inner life, strengthens resilience, and creates clarity in places where confusion once sat. Gratitude is not simply something you feel; it is something you practice, and that practice changes who you become.

Across every domain—business, psychology, faith, philosophy, and leadership—gratitude appears again and again as a foundational principle. I've read an enormous number of books over the years, and no theme is more consistently emphasized than gratitude. Stoic writers highlight it as a mental discipline. Spiritual writers treat it as alignment with truth. Success literature treats it as the doorway to momentum and opportunity.

The Scientific Anchor: Gratitude as a Neuro-Shift

Gratitude earns the title of "superpower" because it is a disciplined practice that actively shifts your brain's chemistry and structure. Decades of research by experts like Dr. Robert Emmons, the world's leading scientific expert on gratitude, confirm this. Through long-term studies, Emmons's work demonstrates that consistent gratitude practice leads to:

- Lowered Cortisol: Reduction in stress hormones, directly counteracting the anxiety induced by the modern, overstimulated world.

- Increased Dopamine and Serotonin: These "feel-good" neurotransmitters increase motivation and stabilize mood, reinforcing the "Reset" discussed previously.

- Improved Sleep and Energy: Grateful individuals report better sleep quality and higher levels of energy, directly fueling the physical capacity needed for sustained learning.

Furthermore, Dr. Martin Seligman, a founder of Positive Psychology, has shown that simple, directed gratitude exercises can measurably increase happiness and decrease depressive symptoms for months. For the learner, this isn't about fleeting joy; it's about building a sustainable emotional baseline that can handle the resistance required for growth. If you want your brain to run a higher operating system, you must supply it with gratitude. It is the cheapest, most accessible, and most powerful form of mental hygiene available.

The Disarming Agent: Envy and Ego

The deepest power of gratitude lies in its ability to disarm the two greatest internal enemies of the disciplined learner: Envy and Ego.

1. Disarming Envy: Envy is the perspective that what you don't have is more valuable than what you do have. It destroys

contentment and makes disciplined effort feel pointless. Gratitude acts as a direct counter-paradigm, forcing the mind to dwell on abundance and stewardship rather than lack. It is impossible to feel deeply grateful and intensely envious at the same moment.

2. Disarming Ego: Ego convinces the learner that their success is entirely their own doing and that they have nothing more to learn. This fragile, self-centered paradigm immediately halts growth. Gratitude, by its very nature, is a confession that you received help, favor, or gifts you did not earn, thereby shrinking the ego and creating space for continued learning.

The Resilience of Kintsugi

The Japanese art of Kintsugi—meaning "golden joinery"—is a powerful, non-personal story that illustrates the resilience of gratitude. When a piece of pottery breaks, Kintsugi masters do not discard it. They repair the crack with lacquer dusted or mixed with powdered gold. The philosophy is that the piece is not ruined; it is more beautiful and more valuable for having been broken. The flaws and the repair become part of the object's history, highlighted with gold rather than hidden.

This is the work of gratitude on the soul. It forces you to look at the broken places—the failures, the setbacks, the moments of personal weakness—and instead of being defined by them, you consciously choose to see the resilience, the lesson, and the strength that emerged from the repair.

I remember a season in my business when a major project failed. It wasn't just a loss of money; it was a public failure that bruised my reputation. For weeks, I felt defeated, trapped in a paradigm of failure and bitterness. One morning, I sat down and forced myself to write a list of everything I still had: a supportive family, the intellectual capital I had gained from the loss, and the clear knowledge of exactly what not to do next time. I saw the broken project not as a closed door, but as a clear-out. The act of giving thanks—even for the knowledge gained in the failure—was the only thing that restored my mental energy and allowed me to move forward. The door was broken, but my ability to walk through a new one was not. That is the resilience gratitude provides.

The learner understands that gratitude is not a denial of difficulty; it is the strategic refusal to allow difficulty to become a defining difficulty. It is the conscious choice to center on the abundance of potential and the clarity of purpose that remains, regardless of external circumstances.

Gratitude is the lens that converts what you have into what you need. It stabilizes identity, inoculates the soul against the temptation of envy, and ensures the learner remains humble enough to keep receiving and keep growing. It is the highest form of thought because it is the most disciplined form of alignment.

My Personal Journey with Gratitude Journaling

Gratitude has always been a kind of superpower in my life. I have leaned on it through some of life's most difficult seasons, something I picked up early in life. But journaling—the practice that so many people talk about as life-changing—was something I could never consistently pull off. I believed in the benefits. I understood the logic. And yet I failed at it countless times. I rarely made it past the five-day mark and never once made it to a full month. Not once.

What finally changed everything for me was lowering the floor so far down that I couldn't talk myself out of it. I made a simple commitment: three things I was thankful for. That was it. No essays. No reflections. No perfect handwriting. Just three specific items every day. I picked up an empty journal (from a bookshelf full of them) and made a commitment. I told myself I would finish that one journal from start to finish, and started writing.

Something shifted almost immediately. Those three small entries began expanding into full pages. The habit grew because my perspective changed. I stopped treating journaling as a task and began treating my day as material. I walked through life looking for things I could write down the next morning—moments I would've missed had I not been searching for them. That shift alone made me more present, more grounded, and more aware of where joy actually hides. Gratitude didn't just brighten my day; it sharpened my attention and made life feel more alive.

And eventually, journaling became more than gratitude. Gratitude stayed the foundation—it's still the requirement—but the journal evolved into something deeper. It became a place to work out the internal battles that don't announce themselves: the boxing matches in my head, the difficult decisions that weigh on me, the anxieties that surface for no obvious reason. When I write, the noise untangles. Thoughts that feel overwhelming in my mind look solvable on paper. A problem that feels like a mountain becomes a sequence of steps. A fear that feels defining becomes something I can name—and once I name it, it loses its authority.

That combination—the discipline of gratitude and the space to think through the hard things—became a turning point for me. The journal is no longer a chore I fail at. It's a tool I rely on. It makes me more present, more grateful, and more capable of navigating the complexities that come with leadership, fatherhood, faith, and life. Gratitude opened the door, but the habit of writing keeps me steady.

Recommended Book

Thanks! How the New Science of Gratitude Can Make You Happier — Robert A. Emmons
The definitive scientific work on the psychological, emotional, and neurological power of gratitude. Emmons demonstrates how directed gratitude reshapes attention, strengthens resilience, and stabilizes the mind for disciplined learning.

CHAPTER 9

Humility: The Strength Beneath All Growth

"Humility is not thinking less of yourself,
it's thinking of yourself less."

— C.S. Lewis

Humility is the virtue that preserves all others. Without it, discipline turns into pride, knowledge turns into arrogance, and purpose becomes a fragile construct tied to your own ability. The learner can absorb every strategy in this book—master focus, embrace difficulty, and frame purpose—but if they lack humility, their growth will inevitably halt at the first plateau of success.

Humility is not self-deprecation. It is the clarity of seeing yourself as you are: a person of immense potential who is simultaneously unfinished. It is the intellectual and spiritual honesty to acknowledge both your gifts and your gaps. This honesty is the engine of all growth because it creates the necessary space for learning. If you believe you are already complete, the book closes.

The Paradox of Level 5 Leadership

In his seminal business research, author Jim Collins defined the concept of Level 5 Leadership—the highest level of executive capability. He discovered that the leaders who built companies from "Good to Great" all shared a paradoxical combination of traits: fierce professional will and profound personal humility.

Their professionalism meant they were ruthlessly committed to the success of the company; they were driven, disciplined, and demanded results. Their personal humility meant they rarely spoke about themselves, deflected praise, and never believed they were bigger than the company. This blend is the essence of the disciplined learner: they possess the professional will to push for mastery and the personal humility to know they are always a student. The humble leader points to a higher standard; the arrogant leader points to themselves.

The Illusion of Knowledge: Dunning-Kruger

The opposite of humility is the destructive mental trap of hubris, often explained by the psychological phenomenon known as the Dunning-Kruger Effect. Ego is not your friend. Ego is the guy at the gym who skips leg day but spends twenty minutes flexing in the mirror. He looks strong, but he can't actually lift anything heavy. This cognitive bias demonstrates that unskilled people often suffer from illusory superiority, overestimating their ability in a given task because they lack the necessary knowledge to accurately assess their own incompetence.

The effect is deadly for a learner. A small amount of knowledge—enough to make a person feel confident—can be the exact thing that stops their development. They become "unconsciously incompetent," not realizing they have vast blind spots. Humility acts as the corrective lens, forcing the learner into a position of conscious, continuous incompetence. The most brilliant people are often the most humble because they have enough knowledge to grasp the true scale of what they do not know.

The Story of the Arrogant Engineer

I once advised a startup founder, an engineer who had built a technically brilliant product. He was genuinely intelligent, but his hubris was a tactical liability. He was so convinced his knowledge was supreme that he dismissed every piece of market data and every dissenting opinion from his team as "ignorant." His paradigm was: I am the expert, therefore my plan is perfect. He refused to learn from the field, from his customers, or from people with non-technical business experience. The market inevitably rejected his product, not because it was bad, but because it solved a problem no one was having in the way he thought they should.

His failure wasn't due to a lack of knowledge or discipline; it was a failure of humility. He chose the comfort of his own certainty over the discomfort of learning from those he considered beneath him. The tragedy is that hubris is the only obstacle that cannot be fixed by discipline—it is a closed door to growth that only humility can unlock.

Humility is the strength beneath all growth because it is the courage to be wrong. It is the daily, disciplined decision to prioritize the truth (of your incomplete status) over the feeling (of your own superiority). It enables you to enter any situation with the question, "What can I learn here?" instead of, "What can I prove here?"

When you accept yourself as a work in progress, you free yourself from the tyranny of having to be perfect. You remove the ego as a barrier to receiving input. Humility is how a disciplined learner ensures they never stop learning.

Recommended Books

Good to Great: Why Some Companies Make the Leap... and Others Don't — Jim Collins
Introduces Level 5 Leadership and the paradox of fierce will paired with deep personal humility — a research-backed argument that humility is the single greatest predictor of sustained excellence.

Ego Is the Enemy — Ryan Holiday
A practical, modern examination of how ego sabotages growth, clarity,

and discipline — and why the learner must defeat ego early to stay teachable.

The Imitation of Christ — Thomas à Kempis
A foundational work on interior humility, self-mastery, and the quiet strength that comes from surrendering ego. It frames humility not as weakness but as the essential disposition for becoming a disciplined, teachable, and grounded human being.

The Skill of Self-Talk: Mastering the Internal Narrative

CHAPTER 10

> *"If you hear a voice within you say*
> *'you cannot paint,' then by all means paint*
> *and that voice will be silenced."*

— Vincent van Gogh

The most important conversation you have every day is the one you have with yourself. This internal dialogue—the voice of the critic, the planner, the judge, and the advocate—is the operating system of your self-belief. It determines the quality of your focus, the resilience of your recovery from failure, and the courage you can muster in the face of fear.

For the disciplined learner, this self-talk is not merely background noise. It is a Skill that must be mastered, because it is the frontline defense against the mental softness diagnosed in Part I. When your inner voice defaults to anxiety, doubt, or avoidance, the entire L-OS slows down. But when that voice is deliberately trained for strength and clarity, it becomes an engine for growth.

This chapter introduces the discipline of internal control, positioned right after Humility. Humility checks your ego. Self-talk mastery ensures you don't overcorrect and let the inner critic destroy your confidence.

The Core Mechanism: Narrative and Identity

Your internal narrative dictates your identity. Most people allow a passive, defeatist story to play on repeat: I am an inconsistent person. I am bad at math. I'm not qualified for this. These are not facts; they are old, unexamined Paradigms that the mind uses to predict the future.

The disciplined learner understands that the goal is not to eliminate negative thoughts but to replace the narrative. You cannot delete a negative thought, but you can always counter it with a superior truth. The conversation shifts from:

Old Narrative: "I failed that test, so I'm not smart enough."

New Narrative: "I failed that test, which is a data point. My identity is a learner, and my job is to find the mistake and correct it. My competence is a function of my effort."

Every time you consciously choose the new narrative, you are performing a mental repetition that strengthens your belief in your capacity for Self-Efficacy.

The Tool: Reframing and Cognitive Restructuring

Psychology provides clear tools for this mastery, particularly in the practice of Cognitive Restructuring (a core component of Cognitive Behavioral Therapy). This technique forces the mind to stop reacting to the emotion of the thought and to instead challenge the evidence behind it.

When the inner critic speaks:

1. Identify: Pinpoint the exact thought (e.g., "This project will fail just like the last one did.").

2. Challenge: Ask disciplined questions: Is this 100% true? What evidence supports this claim? What evidence contradicts it?

(The previous failure bought knowledge, not a guarantee for the next one).

3. Replace: Substitute the emotional thought with a rational, action-oriented statement: "My anxiety is high, which is a signal of importance. I will focus on the next manageable step, which is designing a better test, leveraging the lessons from the last one."

This is Courage in Action. Courage is not the absence of the critic's voice; it is the discipline of proceeding with the better narrative despite the voice's insistence.

The Story of the Two Runners

In the world of ultra-endurance running, the difference between success and failure is often mental, not physical. An experienced runner described his encounter with two different athletes hitting the inevitable "wall" of physical pain and doubt.

The First Runner's self-talk was focused on the pain: "I can't feel my legs. This is misery. I have to stop." He surrendered quickly. His narrative was focused on the external physical feeling.

The Second Runner, in nearly identical pain, had a dramatically different internal conversation. His self-talk was focused on control: "This pain is data. It is a temporary feeling. I will only focus on the next three steps. I choose my steps, not my feelings." He was able to push for hours longer.

The pain was the same. The difference was the Skill of Self-Talk. The successful runner used his internal narrative to reframe the pain as a controlled variable—a temporary cost of the journey—not an absolute, identity-level barrier. He won because he mastered the architecture of his own mind.

The disciplined learner treats their self-talk like a precious input. You must monitor it, filter it, and deliberately rewrite it. Your internal words are the commands the rest of your nervous system must obey. The mastery of your life begins with the mastery of your internal language.

Recommended Books

Beyond Positive Thinking: A No-Nonsense Formula for Getting the Results You Want — Robert Anthony
A direct, practical guide to rewiring the internal narrative, breaking destructive thought patterns, and installing a stronger, more disciplined internal voice.

Daring Greatly — Brené Brown
Explores vulnerability, courage, and emotional honesty — providing deep insight into the shame, fear, and internal narratives that prevent disciplined growth.

PART

RECLAIMING THE LOST ART

The first two parts of this book were dedicated to diagnosis and foundation: resisting the drift of the modern world and constructing the inner architecture of a learner's identity. With the L-OS core virtues—purpose, humility, and courage—now firmly in place, the work shifts from who you are to how you engage with the world. This transition is critical. It is the disciplined application of the self to the flood of information that defines our age. This part is about actively forging a capable mind by recovering the essential cognitive disciplines required to convert consumption into wisdom.

The modern age has made information frictionless and thinking optional. To reclaim the lost art is to choose the path of deliberate mental friction: demanding depth where others settle for shallow scrolling, forcing synthesis where others rely on surface recognition, and cultivating relentless curiosity where others accept easy answers. These chapters are the practical roadmap for mastering your attention, integrating your knowledge, and building the structural memory that ensures your learning is not just absorbed but owned.

Identity in Motion: Consistency as Character

CHAPTER 11

"Every action is a vote for the type of person you wish to become."

— James Clear

Identity is not discovered—it is built. You become who you are by what you repeatedly do. A single decision can shape a moment, but repeated decisions shape a life. Consistency is not merely a habit; it is a form of self-creation. It is how identity moves from idea to evidence.

This chapter stands at the crossroads between your inner architecture and the practices that bring that architecture into the world. It bridges the gap between who you say you want to be and who your life proves you are becoming. Without consistency, everything built internally remains theoretical. Without consistency, purpose weakens. Without consistency, learning collapses into consumption.

Consistency is character in motion. It is the outward expression of the virtues that stabilize the inner life—humility, purpose, and gratitude—made tangible through action.

The Core Mechanism: Identity-Based Habits

As modern habit expert James Clear argues, true change is not outcome-based, but identity-based. Most people focus on the outcome ("I want to write a book"), which requires immense willpower that eventually runs out. The disciplined learner focuses on the identity ("I am a writer"), which changes the motivation source.

When you believe your actions are simply what that kind of person does, the effort required drops dramatically. The daily act of reading is no longer an item on a to-do list; it is a vote cast for the person you have already decided to be. The daily act of resisting distraction is not self-denial; it is an affirmation of the person who values focused learning over fleeting stimulation.

Consistency, therefore, is the act of proving your identity to yourself, over and over, until the new self-image solidifies. It turns an aspirational trait into an axiomatic truth.

The Unseen Power: The Compound Effect

The human mind is terrible at grasping the power of small, consistent effort—the power of marginal gains. This power is known as the Compound Effect. When you commit to a small, 1% improvement in your learning or discipline every day, the result is not a linear progression; it is exponential.

The difference between reading ten pages a day and zero pages a day seems insignificant for a month. But over a year, the ten-pages-a-day learner has consumed 3,650 pages, or roughly 12 to 15 books. They haven't just accumulated information; they have rewired their brain, deepened their paradigm, and strengthened the internal musculature of focus and patience. The consistent, small action, done in private, is what leads to the massive separation that eventually becomes visible in public. Consistency makes effort effortless and growth inevitable.

The Chain of Creation: Seinfeld's System

The power of consistency is best illustrated by the story of comedian Jerry Seinfeld and his system for writing jokes. To ensure he wrote every day—an act of identity formation, not just output—he devised a visual, tangible system known as "Don't Break the Chain."

Every day he spent time writing, he would mark that day with a large red 'X' on a wall calendar. The goal was simple: do not let a day pass without adding an X. The reward was not the joke itself, but the visual chain of completed days. He was not pursuing an outcome (a great joke); he was pursuing a consistent identity (a working comedian). This simple visual accountability loop removed the need for motivation or emotional inspiration. He simply had to protect the chain.

The learner must build their own chain: a small, non-negotiable act that votes for the person they want to be. The power is in the unbroken line, because the chain is not a record of your actions—it is the material evidence of your character.

Consistency is the most authentic expression of self-respect. It says, "I value the vision of who I am becoming enough to show up for myself today." It transforms the theoretical desire to learn into the actual character of a learner.

Recommended Books

Atomic Habits — James Clear
A practical and research-backed framework for building identity-based habits through small, consistent actions. Clearly demonstrates how your habits *are* your identity in motion — perfectly aligned with this chapter's argument that consistency is character expressed daily.

Peak: Secrets from the New Science of Expertise — Anders Ericsson & Robert Pool

A research-backed examination of how deliberate practice builds mastery one incremental improvement at a time. Ericsson reveals why elite performance is not talent but the accumulation of precise, structured 1% refinements — a perfect match for our architecture of progress.

CHAPTER 12

The Student of Everything: Why Lifelong Learners Win

"Go to bed smarter than when you woke up."

— Charlie Munger

L earning for life has never mattered more, and yet fewer people pursue it with seriousness. Real learning—the kind that shapes identity, deepens understanding, and sharpens the mind—has become rare. Information is everywhere, but wisdom is scarce. Opinions are abundant, but discernment is fading. In a world where distraction dominates, the person who commits to lifelong learning immediately gains separation.

Lifelong learning isn't an activity or an academic hobby. It is an identity. It is the internal posture of someone who refuses stagnation and chooses growth. It is the recognition that the mind was designed for expansion, not maintenance. And in a world where many drift passively, the lifelong learner steps forward intentionally.

The Lattice Work of Mental Models

The decisive advantage of the lifelong learner is not specialized knowledge but interdisciplinary perspective. As the investor and thinker, Charlie Munger consistently championed, the best decision-makers don't just know their own field; they have a "lattice work of mental models" drawn from every major discipline: physics, history, psychology, economics, biology, and engineering.

Munger argued that you cannot solve the complex, multidisciplinary problems of the real world with a single disciplinary tool. Instead, you build a mental scaffolding—a lattice work—of core concepts. When a new challenge arrives, the lifelong learner doesn't just ask, "What does my field say?" They ask, "What does the model from psychology say about motivation? What does the model from engineering say about system failure? What does the model from economics say about incentives?"

This creates the "Lollapalooza Effect," Munger's term for when multiple mental models are correctly applied to a single problem, resulting in an explosive, non-linear breakthrough far greater than the sum of the parts. The Student of Everything wins because they are equipped with an intellectual toolkit that allows them to see problems whole, not just in fragments.

The Growth Mindset is the Operating System

This commitment gives a person a decisive advantage. Not because they know everything, but because they live in a constant state of becoming. Lifelong learners adapt faster, see more clearly, and interpret life with greater precision. They enter every season with widening capacity instead of diminishing relevance.

Carol Dweck's work captures this perfectly: growth isn't simply possible— it is natural, if you adopt the mindset that abilities can be developed. A Growth Mindset is not motivational fluff; it is a philosophical posture toward life: I am not finished. I am not fixed. I am not defined by my past ceiling but by my future effort. This is the operating system for the entire Lattice Work. The learner believes their effort—their learning—directly increases their intelligence.

The Story of the Unfinished Symphony

Consider the story of a successful modern entrepreneur who, after struggling with repeated team failures, took a break to study military history and complexity theory. He wasn't seeking business books; he was learning about logistics, command structures, and how complex systems break down in unpredictable ways. He realized the problem wasn't a lack of talent on his team (a fixed paradigm); it was a flaw in his structure of communication and incentive design (a structural, economic model). By applying a mental model from history to a problem in business, he shifted his entire operational strategy and unlocked a period of unprecedented growth.

His success was not an accident. It was the result of his identity as a Student of Everything, willing to look outside his domain for the solution.

The disciplined learner cultivates curiosity, not for trivial entertainment, but for interdisciplinary integration. They know that every new book, every new concept, and every new conversation is another piece of the puzzle. The most powerful ideas are often found outside the traditional boundaries of your work.

This is the ultimate long-term separation that distinguishes the learner. While others stay narrow, reacting to a single dimension of a problem, the Student of Everything brings depth, history, and psychology to the table. They become adaptable, resilient, and virtually indispensable in any environment. They don't just work on their life; they are engaged in the continuous masterpiece of designing their own mind.

Recommended Books

Poor Charlie's Almanack — Charles T. Munger
A masterclass in multidisciplinary thinking, mental models, and lifelong curiosity. Munger reveals why broad learning compounds over time and why those who stay students of everything consistently outperform the specialists around them.

The Fifth Discipline: The Art & Practice of the Learning Organization — Peter Senge

A classic on systems thinking, mental models, and continuous learning. Senge explains how great individuals and organizations grow by constantly expanding their capacity to learn, unlearn, and integrate new ideas.

Mental Craftsmanship: Turning Information Into Wisdom

"The difference between mere knowledge and wisdom is the difference between knowing what to do and knowing how to do it in a way that leads to life."

— Thomas Merton

The modern age has solved the problem of information scarcity, but it has created a profound crisis of processing. We drown in data but thirst for insight. The disciplined learner understands that consuming information is effortless, but crafting wisdom is difficult. It requires deliberate effort to turn raw input into a refined, integrated mental model that changes behavior. This is the work of Mental Craftsmanship.

Mental craftsmanship is the discipline of creating internal structure. It is the active, high-friction process of moving knowledge from mere recognition (the passive thought, I know that) to recall and synthesis (the active ability, I can explain and use that). Without this craftsmanship, your mind becomes a cluttered attic of half-forgotten facts and unexamined opinions.

The Two Modes of Engagement

Cognitive psychology clearly distinguishes between two ways a learner engages with knowledge:

1. Passive Consumption: Scrolling, listening to an audiobook at 2x speed, highlighting text without reflection. This mode relies on recognition. It feels easy and productive, but the information is brittle and rapidly decays. It's the illusion of learning.

2. Active Processing: Writing notes in your own words, drawing diagrams, and immediately applying a concept. This mode forces recall. It feels difficult and slow, but it builds structural memory and integrates the new information into your existing mental model (Paradigm Mastery).

The difference between the learner and the consumer is that the consumer asks, "How much did I read?" The craftsman asks, "How much did I process and synthesize?"

The Feynman Technique: Explaining to Master

The Nobel Prize-winning physicist Richard Feynman developed a foundational technique that perfectly captures mental craftsmanship. The Feynman Technique is a brutal, simple, four-step process for turning information into undeniable understanding:

1. Identify: Choose the concept you are trying to learn.

2. Explain: Write down the concept as if you are teaching it to a ten-year-old. Use simple, non-technical language.

3. Refine: Identify the gaps in your explanation. Where did you rely on jargon or get stuck? Go back to the source material to reinforce that area.

4. Simplify: Rewrite the explanation until it is perfectly clear and concise.

This process ensures you cannot fake understanding. It reveals the exact points where your knowledge is weak, forcing a high-friction engagement with the material that builds structural wisdom. It moves the knowledge from an external resource to an internal, usable tool.

The Art of Synthesis: Leonardo's Legacy

History's greatest learners were not just consumers; they were prolific craftsmen. Consider Leonardo da Vinci. His famous notebooks were not passive journals; they were laboratories of synthesis. Da Vinci wasn't just recording observations in engineering, human anatomy, and botany. He was physically and visually integrating them, drawing connections between the flow of water and the flow of blood, or between structural architecture and natural forms. The sheer act of externalizing his thoughts through drawing, labeling, and writing in multiple domains was the work of synthesis.

The modern learner must adopt this same physical craftsmanship. Wisdom is not stored digitally; it is an internal process that must be externalized. It involves writing, mapping, drawing, and articulating. It requires you to make your learning physical—to force the friction of creation.

Mental craftsmanship is the deliberate refusal to be a passive consumer of information. It is the work of transforming data into integrated wisdom that guides action. By applying friction, forcing recall, and synthesizing concepts across disciplines, the learner ensures that the pursuit of knowledge is an act of creation—and that the mind is always being shaped into something stronger, clearer, and more capable.

Recommended Books

Make It Stick: The Science of Successful Learning — Peter C. Brown, Henry L. Roediger III, Mark A. McDaniel

The definitive work on how real learning happens. This book breaks down why passive consumption fails and how retrieval, spacing, and productive struggle lead to durable wisdom.

CHAPTER 14

Curiosity: The Engine of Mastery

"I have no special talent.
I am only passionately curious."

— Albert Einstein

Curiosity is not a mood or a preference. It is not a personality quirk reserved for the eccentric or the naturally inquisitive. Curiosity is a discipline — a chosen posture toward the world that pulls a person toward growth rather than comfort, toward depth rather than drift, toward meaning rather than distraction. It is the steady willingness to lean forward into the unknown instead of retreating into the familiar.

In a culture dominated by comfort, overstimulation, and passive consumption, curiosity is a radical act. It pushes against the gravitational pull of ease. It interrupts the temptation to settle for shallow novelty. It keeps the mind alive in an environment designed to sedate it. Curiosity is the antidote to intellectual laziness and the spark that ignites mastery.

This chapter builds directly on the previous one. If thinking is the craftsmanship of the mind, then curiosity is the fuel that powers that craftsmanship. Thinking gives form; curiosity gives movement. Thinking deepens; curiosity widens. Thinking refines; curiosity searches. Together, they create the interior engine of a learning life.

The Scientific Anchor: Information Gap Theory

Curiosity feels magical, but it operates on a precise cognitive mechanism, defined by behavioral economist George Loewenstein as the Information Gap Theory. Loewenstein argued that curiosity is not sparked by total ignorance. Instead, it is the feeling of deprivation that comes from perceiving a gap between what we know and what we want to know. This gap creates a state of internal tension, which the brain is motivated to relieve—not with an instant dopamine hit, but with deep, focused learning.

The disciplined learner understands this: you must first build enough foundational knowledge (through consistent action and mental craftsmanship) to recognize the information gap. Curiosity is not a starting point; it is a point of progress. Only the focused mind can generate the powerful, specific questions that unlock true mastery.

Two Kinds of Curiosity: Diversive vs. Epistemic

Not all curiosity is created equal. The modern world offers an endless stream of easily satisfied, low-value information, leading to the first kind:

1. Diversive Curiosity: This is the shallow seeking of novelty. It is the idle browsing of social media feeds, the passive consumption of trivia, or the constant channel-surfing. It is an attempt to escape boredom, but it does not lead to understanding. This is a form of learned distraction (Part I).

2. Epistemic Curiosity: This is the disciplined pursuit of a deep, coherent understanding of a specific topic. It is the intellectual rigor that drives a person to ask why, and then why again. This high-friction curiosity demands synthesis and strengthens the commitment to mastery. It is the kind of curiosity that creates value.

The ultimate goal of the disciplined learner is to starve their Diversive Curiosity and feed their Epistemic Curiosity.

The Engine of Innovation: The Polaroid Story

The power of Epistemic Curiosity is best illustrated by its role in innovation. In 1943, the scientist and inventor Edwin Land was on vacation when his young daughter, Jennifer, asked a simple question after he took her picture: "Daddy, why can't I see the picture now?"

This was not a trivial question. It was a perfect, deeply curious question that exposed a fundamental, unchallenged paradigm in photography. Everyone in the field simply accepted the waiting period. Land, a true Student of Everything, allowed the question to create a massive Information Gap in his mind. He spent the next three years working relentlessly to solve a problem the market hadn't even identified, resulting in the creation of the Polaroid instant camera.

Land's success was not a stroke of genius but a victory of disciplined curiosity. He refused to accept the current limitations of the system, and his simple, profound "why" question served as the engine for a technological revolution.

The disciplined learner must cultivate this kind of internal questioning. You must resist the urge to merely know what something is and instead demand to know why it is that way. Curiosity is the quiet, internal rebellion against the accepted status quo. It is the engine that drives your mind forward, ensures you never reach a final conclusion, and makes the pursuit of mastery an endless source of joy and energy.

G.K. Chesterton saw this clearly when he wrote, "We are perishing for want of wonder, not for want of wonders." The world overflows with things worth exploring, understanding, and interpreting. The problem is not scarcity of material — it is scarcity of attention and the lack of deep, intentional curiosity.

Recommended Books

Curious: The Desire to Know and Why Your Future Depends on It — Ian Leslie

A clear, engaging exploration of how curiosity functions, why it declines in adulthood, and how disciplined inquiry drives innovation, mastery, and a meaningful intellectual life.

IV

THE DISCIPLINE OF CHALLENGE

The path to mastery is paved with resistance, and the modern disciplined learner must not merely survive difficulty but actively grow stronger from it. This section is the L-OS Antifragility Playbook, designed to transition the internal virtues you've built into a durable, shock-proof capacity. It begins with The Skill of Noticing, teaching you to perceive the subtle, high-value data others miss, which is the prerequisite for effective action. From there, you will learn to treat Failure and Difficulty not as threats to be avoided, but as strategic tuition payments that force structural and intellectual upgrades. This is the discipline of becoming Antifragile: the ability to emerge from volatility more capable than you were before the challenge began.

To sustain this high-friction growth, the final chapters provide the necessary guardrails. They introduce the disciplines of protecting your time and energy from the world's demands. You will master The Anti-Schedule to defend the deep, focused time required for creation, and you will learn The Discipline of Rest, understanding that high-quality recovery is not passive reward but an active cognitive tool that consolidates learning and fuels neuroplasticity. The ultimate challenge is not what you do when you are working, but the disciplined structure you build to sustain the work for a lifetime.

The Skill of Noticing: Seeing What Others Miss

CHAPTER 15

"You become what you give your attention to."

— Epictetus

T he mind grows through attention. The learner grows through awareness. And mastery begins long before practice—it begins with noticing.

Noticing is the final internal discipline of the learning-oriented life. If deep work is the forge and curiosity is the spark, then noticing is the quiet skill that sharpens everything. It is the difference between drifting through life and perceiving the truth beneath its surface. It is the difference between reacting and understanding, between consuming and interpreting, between living on autopilot and living awake.

This chapter sits intentionally at the hinge between the inner architecture of the learner and the external mechanics of mastery that follow. The previous chapters provided the internal framework (purpose, humility, gratitude). Noticing is the practice that makes that framework operational.

Thick vs. Thin Description

The academic world has long distinguished between surface-level observation and deep, contextual awareness. Anthropologists call this the difference between Thin Description and Thick Description.

- Thin Description is simply reporting the facts: A person blinked.

- Thick Description is interpreting the context, the meaning, and the systems at play: A person blinked, which suggests anxiety about the upcoming negotiation, indicating their stated position is likely fragile.

Most people operate entirely in the thin. They see an obstacle, but they don't see the lesson embedded within it. They hear a word, but they don't hear the emotion behind it. They look at a business problem, but they don't see the underlying incentive structure causing the issue.

The disciplined learner trains themselves for the thick. They are not merely observing; they are interpreting with the full weight of their cultivated mental models. They know that the most valuable information is rarely loud; it is subtle, hidden in the periphery, and accessible only to the mind.

Noticing as Pattern Recognition

Noticing is the gateway to Pattern Recognition. Your mind is not a storage unit; it is a pattern-finding engine. The more consistently you gather high-quality data (through deep work and epistemic curiosity), the more quickly you recognize deviations from the norm.

This is the competitive advantage. Most people wait for a problem to become a crisis before they react. The learner notices a small anomaly —a shift in a client's tone, a minor inefficiency in a system, a repetitive bad habit—and corrects it before it compounds into a large failure. They see the beginning of the curve, not just the dramatic end. This skill is how a person gains clarity in a noisy world.

The Story of Newton's Apple

The classic image of Isaac Newton and the apple perfectly illustrates the disciplined mind's ability to turn common observation into profound insight. The popular telling suggests the apple simply fell and Newton instantly discovered gravity. But apples had been falling for millennia. The key was not the event but the quality of the observation and the question it generated.

Newton didn't just notice the apple falling. He noticed the problem that had previously been invisible: If this apple falls to the earth, why doesn't the Moon also fall to the earth? His disciplined mind—already filled with a "lattice work of mental models" from mathematics and astronomy—turned a mundane, Thin Description fact into a paradigm-breaking, Thick Description question. The resulting work was not a function of new data but a function of superior observation and interpretation of the data that was already there.

The skill of noticing is the discipline of treating every moment as a laboratory. It is the refusal to accept the superficial explanation. It forces the learner to slow down and create space for the subtle details that reveal the truth. By training yourself to see what others miss, you step out of the chaos of reacting to the surface and into the clarity of understanding the underlying system. You gain the quiet, invaluable advantage of perception.

Recommended Books

The Art of Sticking to It — Bjoern Thelemann
A practical guide to cultivating stillness, clarity, and deep attention in an overstimulated world—training you to notice subtle patterns, details, and truths most people overlook.

The Structure of Scientific Revolutions — Thomas S. Kuhn
A landmark work explaining how breakthroughs come from seeing

anomalies others miss, making it a perfect companion for a chapter on pattern recognition and deep observation.

CHAPTER 16

The Discipline of Challenge: Growth Through Difficulty

"What is to give light must endure burning."

— Viktor Frankl

To grow in any meaningful way, a person must learn to relate to difficulty differently than the modern world encourages. We live in an age built around the removal of friction. Comfort is engineered into every corner of life, and while comfort has its place, it quietly weakens the very systems—mental, emotional, physical—that once made humans adaptable and resilient. The assumption beneath modern convenience is that the good life is the easy life. But anyone who has seriously pursued growth knows the opposite is true: meaningful change requires resistance, pressure, and challenge.

This chapter signals a turning point in the book. Until now, the work has been interior—identity, paradigm, thinking, curiosity, noticing. But interior virtues only matter when they are tested externally. Character matures when it meets resistance. Insight deepens through difficulty. The ultimate discipline is not merely doing hard things; it is creating a strategic system for engaging with the hard things life forces upon you.

The Antifragile Advantage

The goal of the learner is not simply to be resilient. Resilience means you can withstand a shock and return to your original state. The modern thinker and statistician Nassim Nicholas Taleb coined the term Antifragility to describe something that goes beyond resilience: it gets stronger from disorder, volatility, and stress.

In the same way that a muscle fiber tears under stress only to repair itself and grow stronger, the human soul must encounter stress to expand its capacity. The challenge of this discipline is to ensure you treat every setback, failure, and period of difficulty as a positive signal for growth. The disciplined learner doesn't just survive the shock; they strategically use the shock to upgrade their internal operating system. They become Antifragile.

The Proactive Discipline: Premeditatio Malorum

The Stoics, who were masters of mental preparation, practiced a discipline known as Premeditatio Malorum, or the Pre-Meditation of Evils. This is not morbid worry; it is a strategic exercise in emotional inoculation.

The disciplined learner asks: What is the worst that could happen? Then spends time mentally preparing for it. This practice does two things:

1. Reduces Shock: When a predictable difficulty occurs—a major client leaves, a product fails, a key team member quits—the emotion is significantly muted because the mind has already processed the possibility.

2. Forces Strategy: By walking through the malorum (the bad event), you move immediately from emotional reaction to strategic thinking: If this happens, what is my first action? Who do I call? What is the pivot?

This discipline ensures that difficulty, when it arrives, finds you prepared, not panicked. You spend your energy on the solution, not the surprise.

The Story of the Pivot

A prime example of this Antifragility is the early history of the now-massive gaming company Nintendo. When its first foray into electronic entertainment—a laser tag-like system called the Nintendo Beam Gun—was a total, immediate failure, the company did not collapse. The core team did not blame the market or retreat to comfort. Instead, they performed a strategic deep dive (a learning session) on the precise reasons the product failed to gain traction.

They recognized the flaw was a paradigm error: they had built a high-cost product for the luxury consumer market, which they did not understand. They used the severe financial stress of that failure to pivot their entire focus to building a high-volume, low-cost microcomputer called the Famicom (the basis for the Nintendo Entertainment System). The stress of the Beam Gun failure did not break them; it forced a paradigm shift and a strategic refinement that led to one of the biggest commercial successes in history. The discipline of challenge made them stronger than they were before the difficulty occurred.

The greatest growth in your life will always be preceded by a period of intentional or forced difficulty. The disciplined learner views challenge not as a sign that they are on the wrong path, but as proof they are engaged in the process of scaling up. You cannot grow in a vacuum. You grow through tension. You grow when you welcome the pressure, interpret the lesson, and deliberately use the shock to become something more capable, more purposeful, and more robust than your former self.

Recommended Books

Antifragile: Things That Gain from Disorder — Nassim Nicholas Taleb
A powerful examination of how systems—and people—become stronger

through stress, uncertainty, and volatility, aligning perfectly with the chapter's philosophy of using challenge as fuel.

The Saving Power of Suffering: Finding Meaning, Strength, and Redemption in the Cross — Fr. Jacob Powell
A profound reflection on how suffering refines identity, deepens virtue, and reveals purpose when embraced with courage and meaning.

The Obstacle Is the Way — Ryan Holiday
A modern, accessible introduction to Stoic principles, showing how disciplined perception and voluntary difficulty transform obstacles into opportunities.

The Beauty
of Failure

CHAPTER 17

"I have not failed. I've just found
10,000 ways that won't work."

— Thomas Edison

In a culture that demands instant results and presents only polished highlights, failure is interpreted as finality, weakness, and shame. But for the disciplined learner, failure is none of these things. It is the most powerful, high-friction, and effective form of education available. Failure is not the opposite of success; it is a prerequisite for success. It is the process by which theory is tested against reality, and the only way a mental map can be corrected.

The disciplined learner does not try to avoid failure; they train themselves to extract maximum value from it. They understand that to fear failure is to fear growth itself.

Failure as the Cost of Tuition

Every significant personal or professional breakthrough carries a hidden cost: a Learning Debt—the necessary tuition paid through mistakes, miscalculations, and incorrect assumptions. This is why attempting something bold often results in an initial setback. The setback is not a sign of your inadequacy; it is the market, the system, or the process handing you the specific, high-value data you needed to succeed on the next attempt.

When you frame failure as a tuition payment, your perspective changes from regret to calculation. Instead of asking, "Why did this happen to me?" you ask, "What did this mistake buy me?" The learner treats failure as an investment in a knowledge asset that their competitors—who are too afraid to try—do not possess.

Intelligent Failure and Psychological Safety

For failure to be productive, it must be Intelligent Failure, a concept formalized by Harvard professor Amy Edmondson. She defines Intelligent Failure as a setback that occurs in the pursuit of a novel goal, which happens in a new market or situation, and which is accompanied by rigorous learning. The key distinction is that Intelligent Failure should be celebrated, while preventable errors (like carelessness or ignoring existing data) should not.

Edmondson's research on organizational success shows that the highest-performing teams are those with Psychological Safety—a culture where it is safe to speak up, admit mistakes, and take calculated risks without fear of punishment. This is the necessary environment for learning. The disciplined learner cultivates this safety within their own mind, allowing themselves to be wrong without letting the inner critic become a tyrant. You must be willing to honestly document your failure, dissect its root cause, and integrate the lesson immediately.

The Edison Principle: Volume of Effort

The story of Thomas Edison's thousands of attempts to create a viable electric light bulb is the ultimate expression of the beauty of failure. Edison's process was not about a single moment of inspiration; it was about relentless, systematic elimination. He embraced a massive volume of failures because he understood that each one was not an outcome but a data point—a step closer to the solution.

When asked about his persistent setbacks, he did not dwell on the mistake. Instead, he maintained the posture of a learner: "I know more about what will not work than I did a week ago." This is the core discipline: maintaining an identity that is committed to learning and execution regardless of the emotional sting of the results. The successful invention was not the work of genius; it was the inevitable product of a superior failure-to-learning loop.

Failure is not a condition to be managed; it is a resource to be leveraged. It is a necessary friction that reveals your true limits, corrects your paradigms, and sharpens your purpose. By choosing to embrace the full learning cycle—effort, setback, analysis, and refinement—the disciplined learner ensures that the greatest setbacks become the moments that set them up for the greatest leaps in growth. The greatest beauty of failure is that it makes the future possible.

Recommended Books

Chasing Failure: How Falling Short Sets You Up for Success — Ryan Leak
A practical, story-driven exploration of why pursuing goals big enough to risk failure leads to breakthrough growth. Leak reframes failure as a strategic advantage — the clearest path to resilience, confidence, and long-term success.

The Fearless Organization — Amy Edmondson
A research-backed look at psychological safety and productive failure. Edmondson shows why environments that allow honest mistakes accelerate growth, creativity, and long-term excellence — perfectly aligned with your reframing of failure as information, not identity.

The Art of Meta-Learning: How to Learn Anything Quickly

CHAPTER 18

> *"Being busy is most often used as a guise for avoiding the few critically important but uncomfortable actions."*

— Tim Ferriss

Most people believe fast learners are gifted. They're not. They're structured.

The ability to learn quickly has nothing to do with IQ and everything to do with how a person approaches the learning process. Some people drift into a new skill and treat effort as strategy. Others treat learning like a craft—something to be dissected, designed, and executed with precision. The difference between those two people is not intelligence. It is Meta-Learning: the art of learning how to learn.

This chapter marks the transition from internal formation (identity, humility, paradigm) to the external, applied mastery of acquiring new skills quickly and efficiently. The goal is no longer simply to be a learner but to be an effective and rapid acquisition machine—the person who can enter any new environment and immediately understand its structure, allowing them to solve the problem of time.

The Three Pillars of Rapid Acquisition

Meta-Learning is the strategic process of eliminating waste and maximizing high-leverage effort. The goal is to strip away the noise and focus on the 20% of information that will deliver 80% of the practical results (the Pareto Principle). This process is built on three pillars:

1. Deconstruction: Break the skill down into its smallest components. Instead of "learn guitar," the meta-learner asks, "What are the 10 most common chords? What are the 5 strumming patterns that cover 80% of pop music?" This is the discipline of noticing applied to the learning process itself.

2. Selection: Identify and select the only necessary resources. Most people spend weeks consuming introductory material; the meta-learner finds the one or two best resources and immediately discards the rest, removing the distraction of choice.

3. Sequencing: Arrange the components in an optimal sequence. Learning is not linear. The meta-learner designs a path that builds upon itself for maximum retention and minimum frustration, focusing immediately on real-world practice, not passive consumption.

The Core Concept: Strategic Practice Over Time

Author and skill-acquisition expert Josh Kaufman demonstrated the power of a structured learning approach by showing that anyone can go from total ignorance to functional competence in a new skill with just 20 hours of focused, deliberate practice. This challenges the widespread assumption that meaningful ability requires 10,000 hours. The truth is simple: the 10,000-hour rule applies to mastery; the 20-hour rule applies to usefulness. One is for elite expertise. The other is for "I need to understand enough about blockchain to sound competent at dinner before the salad arrives." The key is knowing which level of competence you're aiming for.

The deeper insight is that early incompetence is unavoidable. The first few hours of any new skill feel awkward, slow, and discouraging. Most people quit during this phase, mistaking discomfort for inability. But when you commit to 20 focused hours, you push through the psychological "activation energy" and reach a functional level where progress becomes rewarding instead of painful.

This is the structural antidote to drift. Instead of dabbling, hoping, or procrastinating, you give yourself a clear container: a defined block of time, a deliberate strategy, and the expectation that the beginning will feel clumsy. When the frustration shows up—as it inevitably does—you recognize it as part of the process, not proof that you lack talent.

Once the learner reframes the early struggle this way, rapid progress becomes possible. The mind relaxes. Resistance drops. You stop avoiding the work and start engaging with it. By compressing the learning curve through intentional design, you reclaim the hours that most people waste drifting between distraction and half-effort.

This is why Kaufman's framework is so powerful: it removes the mystery from skill acquisition and replaces it with a repeatable, high-leverage process. You don't need years. You need structure, deliberate practice, and the willingness to endure the short, necessary season of not feeling good at something.

The Story of the Emergency Language Learner

Consider a real-world scenario of a diplomat assigned to an urgent mission in a country where English is not spoken. The diplomat does not have years for academic study. They must learn quickly to be effective. Their process is purely Meta-Learning:

- Deconstruction: They break the language into the 500 most common words, the 10 most essential grammatical structures, and the survival vocabulary for their specific mission (negotiation, transport, public address).

- Selection: They ignore all formal literature and focus entirely on high-density audio and spaced repetition flashcards.

- Sequencing: They start speaking and practicing immediately— not for perfection, but for feedback.

The result is not flawless fluency, but functional competence in a compressed timeframe. This person wins not because they have more talent, but because they have a superior strategy for eliminating non-essential information and maximizing their learning time. The skill they are demonstrating is not language acquisition; it is Meta-Learning.

The disciplined learner treats every new skill like a new project. You must apply the same rigor to how you learn as you do to the work itself. Meta-Learning turns you from a passive recipient of information into the active architect of your own knowledge base. It is the ultimate form of leverage: using a better system to achieve superior results with less time and wasted effort.

Recommended Books

The First 20 Hours: How to Learn Anything... Fast! — Josh Kaufman
A practical breakdown of rapid skill acquisition, showing how deconstructing a skill, identifying critical subcomponents, and practicing deliberately accelerate early progress.

The Anti-Schedule: Time Management for the Deep Learner

CHAPTER 19

"If you don't control your time, someone else will."

— Brian Tracy

The most valuable resource for the disciplined learner is not information, money, or talent; it is uninterrupted time. In a world that runs on notifications, meetings, and instant communication, time is the commodity most ruthlessly stolen. Most people manage their time passively, reacting to the loudest request, and their learning—which requires sustained focus—is perpetually sacrificed.

This chapter provides the strategic framework for defending your attention and ensuring your schedule serves your growth, not the drift of others. It moves you from merely managing tasks to managing energy and deep focus. This discipline ensures that the virtues of the L-OS—from Attention to Consistency —have the protected space they need to thrive.

The Core Paradigm: Maker vs. Manager

Programmer and essayist Paul Graham defined a crucial distinction for anyone engaged in creative or deep work: the Maker Schedule versus the Manager Schedule.

- The Manager Schedule: Operates in one-hour increments, optimized for meetings, quick decisions, and shifting tasks. This schedule is reactive and easily disrupted, making true Deep Work (Cal Newport) impossible.

- The Maker Schedule: Operates in multi-hour blocks (a half-day or more) dedicated to focused, high-leverage creation and thinking. It is an intentional, proactive defense of cognitive space.

Most people, even those who work for themselves, fall into the Manager Schedule. They interrupt their Maker work to answer email, check a quick slack message, or attend a meeting, fracturing their attention. The core discipline of the learner is to adopt the Maker Schedule for the hours that matter most, treating that time as a non-negotiable asset.

The Tool: Time-Blocking for Sovereignty

The "Anti-Schedule" is built on the power of Time-Blocking. It is the discipline of planning your schedule by assigning every single task—including learning, deep work, and rest—to a specific block of time. The primary advantage is not efficiency; it is sovereignty.

- The To-Do List Lie: A to-do list is a wish list. It does not account for time, energy, or friction. It only creates a feeling of vague, overwhelming guilt.

- The Time-Block Truth: A time-block forces you to confront reality. It makes you ask, if this task takes two hours, what other task must I move or eliminate? It is a Paradigm Shift where you decide what the most valuable use of your energy is before the day starts, ensuring you execute the priorities of your Purpose over the demands of others.

The Discipline of the Empty Calendar

The most difficult, yet high-leverage, action is to schedule "nothing." You must block time for tasks that yield the highest cognitive return: deep thinking, synthesis, reflection, and skill acquisition.

I have found that the greatest productivity gain is not from adding a task but from canceling one. My most productive weeks are the ones where I ruthlessly block off a full three-hour morning slot every day for Maker Time, with zero meetings, zero email, and zero exceptions. I treat that time block as if it were a high-stakes meeting with a billionaire client—the client is my future self.

The disciplined learner understands that the path to mastery is not a sprint; it is an organized, high-friction, deeply focused application of energy. You must build a schedule that protects your focus from the world and ensures that the most important conversations and the most meaningful work happen first.

Recommended Books

Essentialism: The Disciplined Pursuit of Less — Greg McKeown
A framework for eliminating the trivial, protecting focus, and building a life around only the things that matter most. Essentialism reinforces your argument that disciplined attention—not calendars—creates the margin required for deep learning.

Atomic Time Management — Bernard Roth
A clarity-driven look at choosing the right priorities, protecting energy, and reducing friction so your attention stays aligned with your highest-value goals. A strong complement to your anti-schedule philosophy.

CHAPTER 20

The Discipline of Rest: Why Recovery is a Learning Tool

"The time to relax is when
you don't have time for it."

— Sydney Harris

In a culture that glamorizes exhaustion, rest is often mistaken for laziness. We treat our energy like an endless credit card, perpetually overdrawn, convinced that the disciplined life is the one that minimizes downtime. This is a profound and costly error. Rest is not the absence of effort; it is an active, strategic discipline—a non-negotiable part of the Learner's Operating System (L-OS).

The human mind and body are not machines designed for perpetual motion. They are complex biological systems that require high-quality recovery to consolidate learning, repair tissue, and maintain optimal cognitive function. The quality of your output is directly proportional to the quality of your input and the quality of your recovery. Without disciplined rest, the entire L-OS becomes brittle. Discipline collapses. Focus fragments. And the learning you worked so hard to acquire is lost.

The Core Mechanism: Consolidation and Neuroplasticity

Scientific research is clear: learning does not end when you close the book. The brain consolidates new information, builds neural pathways (neuroplasticity), and links new concepts into the existing mental lattice work during periods of rest and, most critically, during deep sleep.

When you skip rest, you are not just tired; you are sabotaging the entire learning process. The material you worked hard to process remains in short-term, volatile memory, easily corrupted by stress or forgotten entirely. Rest, therefore, is an investment in your future competence. It is the active process by which your brain turns your effort into your skill.

The Discipline of the Dopamine Reset

The modern learner suffers from chronic overload, which is often disguised as chronic exhaustion. The high volume of low-effort stimulation saturates the dopamine system, leading to a baseline state of anxiety, restlessness, and an inability to enjoy true stillness.

The Discipline of Rest forces a necessary Dopamine Reset. This is not simply lying on the couch to scroll social media (which is consumption, not rest). True restorative rest is the deliberate reduction of hyper-stimulating inputs. It involves:

1. Sleep Sovereignty: Treating sleep as a performance-enhancing drug and the primary discipline of the L-OS. It is non-negotiable.

2. Intentional Boredom: Allowing periods of unstructured, time where the mind can wander. This is essential for creative thinking and the synthesis of disparate ideas.

3. Active Recovery: Engaging in low-stakes, low-focus activities that provide emotional or physical restoration (e.g., walking, prayer, reading fiction).

This disciplined withdrawal from stimulation is the only path back to a motivational baseline that can handle the high-friction effort required for growth.

The Story of the Unplugged Innovator

In the world of technology and innovation, there is a common pattern among high-level creators: the breakthrough often occurs not at the desk, but on the walk, in the shower, or during a holiday. The most famous example is Archimedes' "Eureka!" moment—a flash of insight that occurred when his mind was disconnected from the immediate problem.

A contemporary innovator, a software CEO, realized his best strategic ideas always came to him during his mandatory daily one-hour hike in a place with no cellular service. He didn't initially schedule the hike to think—he scheduled it to stop thinking. He realized that his high-level Maker Time was only possible because his Rest Time allowed his subconscious to process complexity and present him with solutions that his focused, analytical mind could not reach.

He treats his walk as a disciplined act of recovery that enables his creativity. He understands that the pressure required to forge wisdom must be followed by a period of release to set the form.

Rest is a powerful tool for the mind. It is the commitment to Consistency applied to your energy reserves. By treating recovery as a sacred discipline—not a reward earned only after exhaustion—the learner ensures their L-OS is not only running efficiently today but will be structurally sound for the decades of growth ahead.

Recommended Books

Why We Sleep: Unlocking the Power of Sleep and Dreams — Matthew Walker
The foundational research on how sleep drives memory, learning, emotional regulation, and long-term cognitive performance. Walker

demonstrates that rest is not optional but the biological core of high-level mental functioning.

Rest: Why You Get More Done When You Work Less — Alex Soojung-Kim Pang
A counterintuitive exploration of how deliberate rest fuels creativity, productivity, and sustained excellence, reinforcing your argument that recovery is a strategic learning tool.

PART

V

MENTORSHIP, RELATIONSHIP, AND TRIBE

The disciplined learner understands that the fastest path to mastery is never a solitary one. Having successfully constructed the inner architecture of the L-OS, the next essential step is to strategically leverage the wisdom and energy of others. This section is dedicated to building the external architecture that multiplies your effort, provides critical resilience, and compresses the time required for growth. It begins with the fundamental shift from fear to Courage and Confidence, recognizing that the greatest breakthroughs require external risk and that confidence is a memory collected from action—not a feeling that precedes it. True growth is not about eliminating mistakes but about borrowing the wisdom of those who have walked the path ahead.

This external focus culminates in the discipline of curating your environment. You will learn to establish a Personal Board of Directors through strategic mentorshlp—gaining decades of insight in an afternoon. More critically, you will master the Law of Averages by choosing the small circle of peers who refuse to settle, whose standard of excellence becomes your new normal. This tribe acts as a non-negotiable defense against drift, ensuring that your purpose is constantly challenged, your focus is protected, and your L-OS remains structurally sound, sustained by the integrity and ambition of the community around you.

Fear, Courage, and Confidence

CHAPTER 21

"Courage is not simply one of the virtues,
but the form of every virtue at the testing point."

— C.S. Lewis

Fear is one of the oldest human experiences and one of the most misunderstood. In modern culture, fear is treated as something to be avoided, minimized, numbed, or rationalized away. But fear's purpose is not to trap us; it is to teach us. It is not an enemy to eliminate but a signal to interpret. Fear marks the boundary between who we are and who we could become. It is the tension between comfort and calling.

Courage only exists because fear exists. If a task carries no fear, it requires no courage. But when something stirs fear within us—risk, vulnerability, responsibility, uncertainty—that is often the clearest sign that the action is meaningful. Fear appears at the threshold of every important decision. It exposes desire. It reveals attachment. It points to the part of ourselves still unformed.

The Illusion of Elimination

The challenge is that fear often disguises itself as wisdom. It speaks in the language of prudence, caution, and protection, convincing the learner that the goal is to wait for fear to subside before acting. This is the great illusion. You will never eliminate fear. The work of the disciplined learner is to understand the nature of fear and to act anyway.

Psychological work by figures like Dr. Susan Jeffers reinforces this: all anxiety surrounding action comes from a fundamental, hidden belief that you cannot handle whatever outcome the action might produce. The cure, therefore, is not a confidence trick but a fundamental shift in identity and discipline: you must build the internal scaffolding to know with certainty that you can handle it. The solution to fear is not courage; the solution to fear is action.

Courage as Alignment

The Stoics were masters of this discipline. They understood that you cannot control the outcome, the difficulty, or the presence of fear itself. You can only control your judgment and your response. Courage, for the learner, is the complete internal alignment that says: I do not control the results, but I control my disciplined effort to pursue what is right.

Courage is simply virtue at the point of action. When you act with integrity despite fear, you build the evidence of who you are. This evidence is what the mind requires to feel confidence. Confidence is not a feeling that precedes action; it is a memory that follows successful action. It is the proof collected by the disciplined self that they are capable of doing hard things.

The Story of the Two Founders

I have watched this play out in business countless times. I know two founders, both brilliant, who had the same idea for a high-risk tech product.

The First Founder spent six months in "analysis paralysis." He feared failure, feared losing capital, and feared public criticism. He told himself he was waiting for the fear to go away, but he was actually waiting for the guarantee of success. The fear never left, and he eventually abandoned the project. His fear was an identity issue: I cannot handle failure.

The Second Founder experienced the exact same fear, but she used it as a compass. She acknowledged the fear and then asked, What is the smallest action I can take right now to gather information? She launched a minimum viable product (MVP) in three weeks, accepted the failure of the initial model, and used the resulting data to pivot. She gained confidence not because she eliminated fear, but because she collected the undeniable memory of having acted through it. Her courage was the conviction that I can handle whatever happens next.

The core lesson for the disciplined learner is simple: Fear is not the enemy of growth; inaction is. Every time you feel the tension of fear and choose to execute the small, deliberate action that aligns with your purpose, you cast a vote for your desired identity. That consistency is what accumulates into genuine, unshakeable confidence. Fear provides the resistance; courage provides the action; and action delivers the confidence to keep learning.

Recommended Books

Feel the Fear and Do It Anyway — Susan Jeffers
A direct, practical framework for understanding fear as a signal—not a stop sign—and building the inner confidence that emerges only through

action. Jeffers aligns perfectly with your theme that courage is the form virtue takes at the testing point.

The War of Art — Steven Pressfield

A sharp, compelling look at the internal resistance that blocks growth and the discipline required to move through fear into purposeful action. A strong companion to your argument that confidence is the byproduct of action, not a prerequisite.

CHAPTER 22

The Power of Mentorship

"To teach is to act with charity."

— Thomas Aquinas

Mentorship is one of the oldest forces for human growth, yet one of the most undervalued in modern life. People often imagine mentors as formal figures—coaches, professors, industry veterans —but true mentorship is far broader. It is the transfer of wisdom across experience. It is what happens when someone who has walked ahead offers insight to someone following the path. The disciplined learner understands that the fastest path to mastery is never solitary; it is always guided.

The goal of the learner is not to avoid mistakes but to make new mistakes. Mentorship is the high-leverage tool that allows you to avoid the painful, costly, and time-consuming errors that your guide has already made. It turns decades of experience into an afternoon conversation, accelerating your growth exponentially.

The Three Dimensions of Guidance

The effective learner builds a comprehensive system of guidance that goes beyond a single formal relationship. They curate a Personal Board of Directors composed of three distinct dimensions of mentorship:

1. Direct Mentorship (The Guide): The living, active guide who is ahead of you, capable of providing direct feedback on your work and life. This person is essential for accountability, navigating specific challenges, and demonstrating consistency.

2. Peer Mentorship (The Iron): The peer-level relationship that provides mutual challenge and accountability. This is the Mastermind Group or the small circle of trusted colleagues who are pursuing excellence alongside you. This relationship protects against the subtle drift of comfort by raising the internal standard of the collective.

3. Intellectual Mentorship (The Giants): The wisdom absorbed from great thinkers, past and present, through books, documentaries, and recorded lectures. This is the most accessible and least utilized form of mentorship. The disciplined learner consciously seeks out the counsel of "giants" (as mentioned in the Introduction) to shape their paradigms and inform their character.

The Power of Asking: The Story of Steve Jobs

The power of seeking out mentorship—even when the guidance seems unattainable—is perfectly illustrated by the story of Steve Jobs and his pursuit of Edwin Land, the inventor of the Polaroid camera.

When Jobs was developing the Macintosh, he was obsessed with the idea of a personal computer that was as beautiful and user-friendly as a work of art. He recognized Land as a historical intellectual mentor who embodied the synthesis of art and science. Jobs simply called Land, who was still alive at the time, and arranged a meeting. Land became a short-term, impactful mentor for Jobs, sharing his perspective on the critical importance of aesthetics and simplicity in product design.

Jobs was not Land's student; he was a disciplined learner who had done his homework and sought out the precise, high-leverage advice he needed from a giant. The lesson is that mentorship is often an act of courage and initiative. The person who asks the best questions usually finds the best guide.

Mentorship as Humility in Action

Seeking a mentor is the ultimate act of humility. It is the acknowledgement that the wisdom you currently possess is insufficient for the growth you desire. The act of asking for help forces the ego to recede and creates the space for new knowledge to enter.

Mentorship is not a dependency; it is leverage. It is how you multiply your efforts and drastically compress the time required to reach a new level of competence. The disciplined learner wins because they understand that they do not have to learn every lesson the hard way. They can borrow the wisdom forged in the fire of someone else's past challenges.

Recommended Books

The Trillion Dollar Coach: The Leadership Playbook of Silicon Valley's Bill Campbell — Eric Schmidt, Jonathan Rosenberg, Alan Eagle
A powerful exploration of how wise mentorship accelerates mastery by collapsing decades into days and sharpening leadership through honest counsel and accountability.

Mastery — Robert Greene
A sweeping study of how the apprentice–mentor dynamic has shaped world-class achievers across history — reinforcing your claim that mentorship multiplies learning.

Choosing People Who Raise Your Standard

CHAPTER 23

"You are the average of the five people you spend the most time with."

— Jim Rohn

After establishing the pillars of a learning identity—purpose, humility, consistency, and a disciplined approach to learning itself—the final external piece is the environment. No person can sustain a high standard of discipline, curiosity, and growth in isolation. The people you choose to surround yourself with are not accessories to your life; they are the external architecture that either supports or sabotages your ambition. They are the gatekeepers of your comfort level.

The person you spend time with dictates the language you speak, the challenges you accept, the excuses you permit, and the ceiling of what you believe is possible. The disciplined learner understands that choosing your "tribe" is not a social decision; it is a strategic decision that determines your long-term identity and success.

The Core Mechanism: The Law of Averages

The most direct articulation of this truth is the Law of Averages, which suggests that your skill, income, mindset, and health will inevitably gravitate toward the average of your closest associates. This is not a moral statement; it is a mathematical inevitability.

When you surround yourself with people whose standards are higher than your own—people who read more, build more, serve more, and think more deeply—their standard becomes your new normal. Their excellence becomes your minimum acceptable threshold. Conversely, when you consistently spend time with those who prioritize comfort, distraction, and pessimism, their lower standard becomes the gravity that pulls your own habits into drift. You do not rise to the level of your goals; you fall to the level of your immediate environment.

The Science of Emotional and Social Contagion

This phenomenon is rooted in the science of Emotional and Social Contagion. Human behavior is highly influenced by proximity. Research has shown that social networks can unconsciously influence everything from happiness and mood to financial decisions and even health habits. When your peers are disciplined learners, their curiosity, humility, and willingness to tackle hard things become subtly contagious.

Your tribe creates a shared, unwritten paradigm about what constitutes "normal effort" and "acceptable failure." By choosing a high-standard tribe, you externalize the hard work of discipline. You rely on their collective integrity to maintain your own. When you feel unmotivated, their energy becomes the bridge that carries you across the gap of your own temporary weakness.

The Inklings: The Power of Shared Standard

The power of a high-standard tribe is beautifully illustrated by the Inklings, a famous informal literary group that met in Oxford throughout the 1930s and 1940s. Its members included some of the 20th century's most profound writers, notably C.S. Lewis and J.R.R. Tolkien.

The Inklings were not mentors to one another in the traditional sense, but they were peer-level companions who existed to hear, critique, and challenge each other's work. They acted as a ruthless intellectual proving ground. It was in this group that the manuscripts for The Lord of the Rings and The Chronicles of Narnia were first read aloud, dissected, and sharpened.

Their combined standard of excellence—their commitment to literary depth, mythic power, and Christian allegory—created an environment where shallow work was impossible. The work of one (Tolkien) inspired the monumental work of the other (Lewis). They were the living proof that when disciplined learners choose to align their purpose, their collective will can lead to world-changing output.

The task of the disciplined learner is not just to filter negative influences but to actively curate positive ones. You must find the people who treat your ambition as normal and your growth as a shared obligation. Choose the voices that speak to the person you are becoming, not the person you have been. The ultimate act of self-authorship is choosing the co-authors of your environment.

The Rarity and Power of a True Circle

One of the greatest competitive advantages a person can have in life is a circle of friends who challenge them, sharpen them, and genuinely want to see them win. Not acquaintances. Not drinking buddies. Not passive friendships built on convenience. I'm talking about a group of people who hold you accountable to your potential, confront you when you drift, and celebrate you without envy when you rise.

Most people have never experienced this. They don't even know it exists.

I consider myself fortunate—and deeply grateful—that I have a large number of men in my life whom I talk to regularly, men who truly want to see me succeed. They push me, question me, pray for me, and tell me the truth even when it stings. They hold me to a higher standard, not because they're hard on me, but because they believe fiercely in the person I'm called to be. And here's the surprising part: this isn't rare because it's impossible. It's rare because most people never go looking for it.

There are countless extraordinary people in the world who are trying to do extraordinary things—but they are invisible to the person who lives passively, clings to comfortable relationships, or surrounds themselves with people who aren't going anywhere. Finding a circle of high-standard friends requires intention. It requires humility. And sometimes, it requires painful decisions.

If you want to attract high-caliber people into your life, you often have to become the kind of person those people want to be around. That means distancing yourself from relationships that pull you backward, dilute your standards, or quietly resent your growth. You don't have to shame those relationships. You don't have to announce anything dramatic. But you do have to recognize that proximity shapes identity. Who you spend time with is who you become.

Great friendships are not an accident. They are built through alignment —shared values, shared pursuits, shared commitment to growth. They are formed over time, tested through difficulty, and strengthened by mutual accountability. And when you experience that kind of community, you understand something most people never discover: your environment is a force multiplier. The right people accelerate your growth more than books, systems, or goals ever could.

If you don't have a circle like this yet, don't assume it's out of reach. Start by becoming someone who lives intentionally, pursues excellence, and genuinely supports others. Seek out people who are building, not drifting. Serve them. Encourage them. Add value to their lives. Over time, you will find that the people who challenge you most are also the ones who lift you highest.

A great circle of friends is rare. It is powerful. And it is absolutely attainable. Don't settle for relationships that keep you comfortable. Build relationships that help you become who you were designed to be.

Recommended Books

The Power of the Other — Dr. Henry Cloud
A deep look at how relationships shape identity, discipline, and the standards you accept for your life.

Boundaries — Henry Cloud & John Townsend
A practical manual for setting relational limits so you can surround yourself with people who elevate your intentions rather than diminish them.

PART

VI

THE CREATOR'S PLAYBOOK

With the internal virtues and external support systems of the L-OS now in place, this section shifts the focus entirely to externalizing wisdom and maximizing output. The goal of the disciplined learner is not merely to be well-read but to be a prolific creator—someone who generates value from their knowledge. This playbook begins with the discipline of efficiency, showing you how to apply the 80/20 Learning Model to ruthlessly filter away non-essential information and focus on the Minimal Effective Dosage that unlocks functional competence in any new domain.

The latter part of the section defines the essential disciplines of creative execution. You will master the Clarity of the Blank Page, understanding that writing is a core Synthesis tool for generating thought and exposing the unexamined flaws in your ideas. This culminates in The Teacher's Test, which positions the act of giving away knowledge—through speaking, teaching, or mentoring—as the final, most rigorous validation of your own mastery, ensuring that your learning always leads to external service and a valuable legacy.

The 80/20 Learning Model: Finding the Minimal Effective Dosage

CHAPTER 24

"Focus on the smallest number of activities that deliver the greatest results."

— Vilfredo Pareto (Adapted)

The biggest illusion in learning is the belief that volume equals value. We assume that if we read more, attend more meetings, or consume more content, we will inevitably become smarter. This is a trap built for mental consumers, not disciplined learners. Time is finite, and the most common cause of intellectual drift is the inability to distinguish between the essential and the noise.

This chapter introduces the fundamental discipline of efficiency: the 80/20 Learning Model. It is the strategic commitment to ruthlessly filter your knowledge intake to focus only on the information that will yield the greatest results. This is how the Learner's Operating System (L-OS) optimizes for speed, clarity, and competence.

The Core Mechanism: The Pareto Principle

The 80/20 Rule, or the Pareto Principle, was discovered by economist Vilfredo Pareto, who observed that 80% of the land in Italy was owned by 20% of the population. This principle has been extended across all domains: 80% of sales come from 20% of clients, 80% of system crashes come from 20% of bugs, and most importantly for the learner, 80% of the usable knowledge in any domain is contained in 20% of the content.

The disciplined learner treats this rule not as an observation but as a mandate for filtering. It forces a necessary Paradigm Shift: the goal is not to finish every book or master every detail; the goal is to identify and master the Minimal Effective Dosage (MED) of knowledge that unlocks functional competence and enables the next stage of growth.

The Discipline of Minimal Effective Dosage (MED)

The MED is the smallest amount of input that produces the desired result. The process of finding it is a form of Meta-Learning built on intentional filtering:

1. Deconstruction: When approaching a new skill, deconstruct it into its smallest, most frequent components (e.g., the 10 most common formulas in a spreadsheet or the 5 most common chords in a song). These components are the 20%.

2. Selection: Ask, "What are the 1-2 books, the 1-2 people, or the 1-2 core concepts that every master of this field must know?" Ignore all other recommended resources until the MED is mastered.

3. Elimination: Identify the 80% of wasted effort: the peripheral theories, the historical context, the niche exceptions. These are saved for later, advanced study. The learner focuses on the center of the target, not the decorative rings.

This process is a fierce defense of Attention. It eliminates the vast majority of low-value content that often occupies 80% of an aspiring learner's time.

The Story of the Language Hacker

The power of the MED is famously demonstrated by modern "language hackers" who can achieve conversational fluency in a new language in a fraction of the time of traditional academic study. Their strategy is pure 80/20.

They ignore thousands of words of vocabulary and months of grammar drills. Instead, they focus relentlessly on the 500 most common words, which account for over 70% of spoken conversation. They memorize a core set of 10 verb conjugations and immediately begin practicing their output.

They do not become scholars of the language, but they achieve their goal: functional competence and communication. They win because they have applied a superior strategic filter to their learning, proving that the focused effort on the essential few always outperforms generalized effort on the non-essential many.

This disciplined filtering is not a shortcut; it is a higher form of intellectual honesty. It requires the courage to admit that you do not need to know everything, but you must master the few things that matter most. The 80/20 Learning Model ensures that your precious time and disciplined focus are dedicated exclusively to building the structural wisdom that will compound into long-term mastery.

Recommended Books

The One Thing — Gary Keller & Jay Papasan
A focused blueprint for identifying the few vital actions that produce disproportionate results — reinforcing your argument that the disciplined learner targets leverage.

Margin: Restoring Emotional, Physical, Financial, and Time Reserves to Overloaded Lives — Richard A. Swenson, M.D.
A Christian-influenced but widely respected book on eliminating overload and restoring the space required for deep work, clarity, and meaning.

The Clarity of the Blank Page: Writing as a Thinking Tool

"I write entirely to find out what I'm thinking, what I'm looking at, what I see, and what it means."

— Joan Didion

The final stage of mental craftsmanship is the willingness to confront the blank page. Most people treat writing as a secondary function—the final step used to communicate an idea that is already fully formed. But for the disciplined learner, writing is a primary tool for thought generation and synthesis. It is the essential friction required to convert vague recognition into concrete, usable wisdom.

The blank page is a laboratory. It is where you isolate your ideas, test their logic, and expose their flaws. If you cannot write a concept down clearly, you do not truly understand it. If you are struggling to write, you are not struggling with writing; you are struggling with thinking.

This discipline is the highest expression of Synthesis. It forces the knowledge acquired into a single, linear, accountable form that must stand up to external critique and internal logic.

The Core Mechanism: Externalizing the Vague

The human mind is an expert in holding vague, incomplete thoughts. We often feel like we understand a concept until we are forced to articulate it. Writing is the mechanism for externalizing the mess.

When you write, you are literally forcing your mind to slow down and translate internal, non-linear thought into external, linear language. This process:

1. Exposes Gaps: The Feynman Technique proves that the gaps in your knowledge become immediately visible when you try to teach or explain. Writing is the ultimate form of self-teaching.

2. Forces Synthesis: When connecting two disparate points from your mental lattice work, writing forces you to build the bridge. It makes you articulate the "why" and the "how" of the connection, transforming a correlation into an insight.

3. Creates Distance: Writing puts your ideas outside of you, allowing you to treat your own thoughts like an artifact to be examined. This distance is essential for objective reflection and for checking your Paradigm.

The Discipline of the Daily Journal

You do not need to write a book or a blog to practice this discipline. A simple, daily commitment to journaling—or the "morning pages" exercise—is enough to strengthen the mental muscle. This is not a passive diary entry; it is an act of courage and humility.

The disciplined writer uses this time to engage in the Socratic Review: What paradigm did I operate from today that caused me friction? What difficult thing did I choose to avoid? What is the clearest articulation of my current purpose?

The act of writing down a problem is the first step toward solving it, because it moves the issue from the overwhelming noise of the mind to the manageable structure of the page. You stop spinning and start linear processing.

The Story of Marcus Aurelius

The timeless work of Marcus Aurelius, the Roman Emperor and Stoic philosopher, is the ultimate testament to writing as a thinking tool. His Meditations (not written for publication) were a series of private, daily exercises in self-correction. He used writing to:

- Check his Morality: Forcing himself to articulate his principles, ensuring his actions align with his philosophy.

- Prepare for Difficulty: Practicing Praemeditatio Malorum by writing down the worst possible events, thus inoculating himself against emotional shock.

- Affirm his Identity: Repeatedly write down his role, his duty, and his virtues.

Aurelius didn't write because he was an emperor with free time; he wrote because writing was the only way to sustain the mental clarity required to govern the world's most powerful empire. His legacy is the proof that the blank page is the ultimate tool for achieving internal mastery.

The disciplined learner chooses the friction of the blank page because they understand that the most valuable ideas are the ones that only they can articulate. Writing is the final discipline that converts knowledge into a profound, usable reality.

Recommended Books

Bird by Bird — Anne Lamott
A reflective, practical guide to writing as a thinking tool — showing how the blank page clarifies ideas, identity, and intention.

The Artist's Way — Julia Cameron
A 12-week journey into creative clarity and disciplined expression, strengthening your argument that writing is a tool for discovery, not perfection.

The Teacher's Test: How to Learn by Giving Away Knowledge

CHAPTER 26

"If you can't explain it simply, you don't understand it well enough."

— Albert Einstein

All learning is a progression toward contribution. The final, high-stakes test for the disciplined learner is not a certification or an exam; it is the moment you must transfer your knowledge to another human being. This is the Teacher's Test.

The ultimate goal of the Learner's Operating System (L-OS) is not personal accumulation but the creation of external value through Service. When you give away your knowledge—whether by teaching a colleague, mentoring a younger person, or writing a clear explanation—you are forced into the most rigorous act of synthesis and clarity. You discover the true depth of your understanding not when you absorb the information, but when you give it away.

The Core Mechanism: The Final Synthesis

Teaching is the highest form of Mental Craftsmanship. It ensures that your knowledge is structurally sound, universally applicable, and free of the vague technical jargon that often disguises shallow understanding.

When preparing to teach, the mind engages in a unique kind of processing:

1. Forced Deconstruction: You must immediately break the concept down into its most fundamental truths.

2. Externalizing the Map: You must translate your personal Paradigm — the way you see the world—into a linear, step-by-step map that another person can follow.

3. Predicting Friction: You must anticipate where the other person will get confused, forcing you to find the strongest metaphors, examples, and analogies.

This entire process is a form of Double-Loop Learning that exposes every weak point in your knowledge. If you are struggling to teach a concept, the struggle is not with the student; it is with the gaps in your own understanding.

The Discipline of the Whiteboard

The most effective tool for this discipline is the Whiteboard Test. Whether real or virtual, the whiteboard forces you to stand opposite your own idea and reduce it to its core structure.

This is the practical application of the Feynman Technique in its highest form: you are not explaining it to yourself; you are explaining it to a living, breathing external mind. The feedback is immediate, merciless, and invaluable. The moment a student asks, "Why is that true?" or "What does that word mean?" your intellectual Humility is immediately checked. Your ego is forced to recede, and your focus shifts entirely to clarity.

The discipline is to seek out the Teacher's Test frequently, to volunteer to teach, to write the explanatory post, to mentor the newcomer.

The Story of the Master Plumber

In any field of mastery, there is a clear distinction between the person who does the work and the person who teaches the work. I once observed an aging master plumber who was capable of fixing any water issue in any building, but he struggled to explain his process to his young apprentice.

He was technically brilliant, but his knowledge was brittle—it only existed in his own head. When he finally forced himself to teach his apprentice the core five principles of a plumbing system (the 20% of the knowledge that solves 80% of the problems), his own speed and efficiency in his daily work increased. By forcing the articulation, he clarified his own process. He became not just a master plumber but a master systematizer of plumbing.

His commitment to teaching was the final act that converted his implicit knowledge (what he could do) into explicit wisdom (what he could reliably transmit).

The disciplined learner understands that the greatest value of their acquired knowledge is realized when it is deployed for the benefit of others. By embracing the Teacher's Test, you ensure your growth is always tied to contribution, your understanding is always rigorously checked, and your legacy is actively being built through the wisdom you give away.

Recommended Books

The Talent Code — Daniel Coyle
An exploration of how teaching, coaching, and shared practice deepen skill, strengthen mental models, and accelerate mastery.

VII

SYSTEMS, HABITS, AND EXECUTION

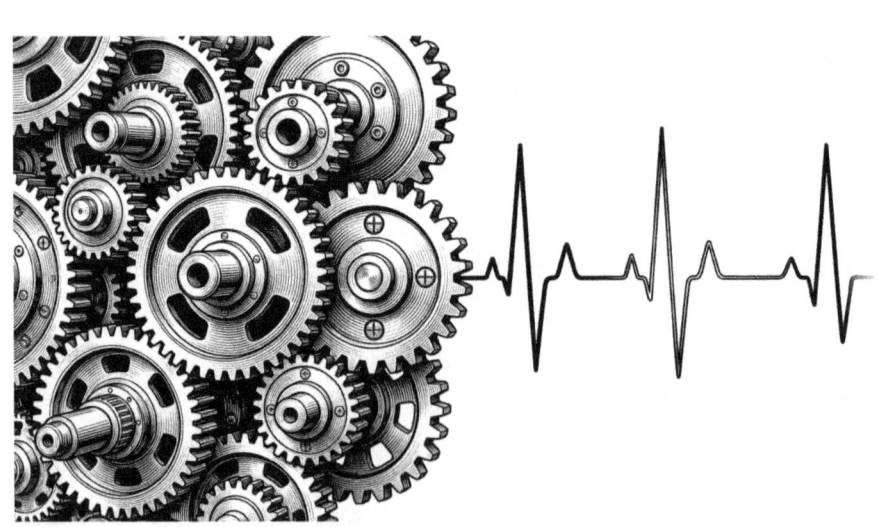

The first six parts of the L-OS established the internal identity and external creative disciplines. This section, the Automation Machinery, is dedicated to eliminating reliance on motivation and making growth a matter of predictable process. You will master the principle of Systems Over Emotion, understanding that a system is a disciplined procedure designed to function irrespective of your mood, energy, or inspiration. This requires mastering the Habit Loop—the neurological cycle that automates high-leverage actions—and applying the science of the Goldilocks Rule to ensure your daily consistency is sustainable and always challenging your current ability. The goal is to build an identity that is structurally sound enough to execute the plan even when the initial passion has faded.

The final disciplines of this Part are dedicated to self-governance and defense. You will learn to use Reflection Without Calendars as the active tool for Double-Loop Learning, ensuring that you are consistently correcting your underlying assumptions, not just your superficial mistakes. This culminates in The Discipline of Say No, the essential security system for protecting your sovereignty. By treating your time and focus as a fixed, sacred resource, you ensure that your disciplined growth is never hijacked by the demands, requests, or noise of the outside world. You build a machinery of execution that is robust enough to carry your commitment across a lifetime.

CHAPTER 27

Systems | Over Emotion

*"You do not rise to the level of your goals.
You fall to the level of your systems."*

— James Clear

E motion is a powerful companion but an unreliable guide. It fluctuates with sleep, stress, circumstance, environment, and even weather. Emotion can ignite action, but it cannot sustain it. It can inspire clarity in one moment and cloud judgment in the next. Anyone who relies on emotion to carry them toward consistency eventually struggles, not because they lack strength, but because they are leaning on something designed to fail them.

This chapter begins Part VI, which takes the virtues and disciplines of the previous sections and turns them into repeatable, long-term machinery. The goal of the disciplined learner is to make growth a matter of process, not willpower. Identity is the map; systems are the vehicle.

The Illusion of Motivation

The most common mistake the aspiring learner makes is waiting for "motivation." They believe they must feel like reading a challenging book, feel inspired to write, or feel energetic to engage in a difficult task. But motivation is not a starting point; it is often a result of action.

Systems eliminate the need for this emotional state. A system is a disciplined procedure designed to function irrespective of your feelings. It is the decision made today that determines the action of tomorrow. It acknowledges that when you are tired, distracted, or discouraged, you will default to the lowest friction activity—and systems are designed to make the productive choice the path of least resistance.

The Science of Friction: The Fogg Behavior Model

The behavioral scientist B.J. Fogg of Stanford University formalized this concept into the Fogg Behavior Model (B=MAP). This model states that a behavior (B) only happens when three elements converge at the same moment: Motivation (M), Ability (A), and a Prompt (P).

Crucially, Fogg demonstrated that when motivation is low (which it often is), the only way to ensure the behavior still happens is to dramatically increase the Ability to do the task, which means reducing the friction or difficulty. This is the core function of a system.

A system is a deliberate, upfront investment of energy designed to reduce the friction of execution:

- Example: Setting out your workout clothes the night before reduces the friction of exercise.

- Example: Keeping your learning materials on the kitchen table reduces the friction of studying.

- Example: Having a dedicated "Deep Work" time slot on your calendar reduces the friction of focus.

The system ensures that the productive task becomes so easy it happens automatically, regardless of whether your motivation is at a 2 or a 10. You win by design, not by desire.

The Story of Twyla Tharp: The Ritual of the Box

The famous dancer and choreographer Twyla Tharp illustrates the power of systems in creative work. Tharp's work requires immense emotional energy, but she does not rely on emotional inspiration to start. She relies on a system.

For every new project, Tharp would start with a ritual: she would take a cardboard box, write the name of the new project on the outside, and place all her initial research, notes, music, and sketches inside. When the box was ready, her first act every day was not to feel creative, but simply to engage with the box. She hired a taxi to drive her to the gym, and this simple, structured action was her "Prompt." The movement, the routine, and the simple act of engaging with the physical system of the box eliminated the crippling emotional friction of the blank page.

Her goal was never to complete the work; it was to not break the system (Consistency). She understood that the final creative output was not the result of a creative spark but the inevitable product of a disciplined process.

Discipline is the mastery of this process. The disciplined learner understands that the greatest tool for consistency is not a stronger will, but a smarter design. By building non-negotiable systems that prioritize high-leverage activities, you make your growth automatic and your long-term success immune to the fluctuations of your daily emotions.

Recommended Books

Work the System — Sam Carpenter
A practical guide to building processes that outperform emotional decision-making — aligning with your call to rely on systems rather than moods.

Switch: How to Change Things When Change Is Hard — Chip Heath & Dan Heath

A research-backed look at how environment and systems shape behavior more reliably than motivation.

CHAPTER 28

Habits That Build a Lifetime

"We are what we repeatedly do.
Excellence, then, is not an act but a habit."

— Aristotle

Greatness rarely comes from a single decision. It almost never comes from a dramatic burst of motivation. Instead, greatness is built slowly—through actions aligned with identity, repeated long after emotion has faded. A strong, clear, purposeful life is constructed through habits.

Habits form the architecture of who you become. They are the daily expression of identity. They support your goals quietly while the world sees only the results. When growth stalls, it is often not because desire is weak but because structure is missing. Emotion cannot sustain what only systems and habits can uphold.

If systems are the framework, habits are the movements that animate that framework.

The Core Mechanism: The Habit Loop

Habits are not mystical; they are neurological cycles that the brain creates to reduce cognitive load. The work of Charles Duhigg formalized this process into the Habit Loop: Cue → Routine → Reward.

1. Cue: A trigger that tells your brain to go into automatic mode (e.g., sitting down at your desk).

2. Routine: The behavior you perform (e.g., opening a challenging book).

3. Reward: The positive reinforcement that tells your brain the routine is worth remembering and repeating (e.g., the feeling of intellectual clarity or marking a chain on a calendar).

The key to building a lifetime of learning is not forcing new routines but mastering the Cues and Rewards and making the productive routine the path of least resistance. The disciplined learner designs their cues to trigger intentional action and their Rewards to reinforce their identity.

The Identity-Habit Feedback Loop

As established, consistency is evidence of character. Habits create a powerful, self-reinforcing loop that solidifies your identity:

1. Identity: I am a learner. (Core Belief)

2. Habit: I read 10 pages before opening my email. (Action)

3. Proof: The habit is performed, casting a vote for the identity.

4. Reinforcement: The identity is strengthened, making the next habit easier.

When you fail to perform the habit, the loop works in reverse, casting a vote against the desired identity. The goal is to accumulate enough successful "votes" until the identity of a focused, disciplined learner becomes an unshakeable, subconscious truth. My mood tells me to hit snooze. My discipline tells me to get up. The truth is, my coffee maker is the most consistent force in my life, and I respect it deeply. It never asks how I feel about brewing.

Sustaining the System: The Goldilocks Rule

Even the most perfectly designed system can fail if the habits are too difficult. Habit formation expert James Clear identified the importance of the Goldilocks Rule: Humans experience peak motivation not when performing tasks that are easy, nor when performing tasks that are overwhelmingly difficult, but when performing tasks that are just right—at the edge of their current abilities.

This rule is vital for long-term consistency. The disciplined learner begins a new habit at a ridiculously small, easy scale (a "Two-Minute Rule" habit). As they master that level, they introduce a small increase in difficulty to keep the challenge "just right." This intentional, gradual scaling ensures that the habit remains sustainable and that the learner is always working in the sweet spot of peak engagement and growth. You must make the habit easy to start but continually challenging to sustain.

The Story of the Daily Writer

The late novelist Anthony Trollope demonstrated the ultimate habit mastery. Trollope was an English post office official who became one of the most prolific writers in history, producing dozens of novels. His success was entirely due to his system. He trained himself to write a fixed number of words every day (approximately 250 words every 15 minutes) and scheduled his writing for the same three hours every morning before his full-time job began. If he finished a novel early, he would immediately move to a blank sheet of paper and begin the next one.

His commitment was not to the emotional state of "being a writer," but to the physical, time-based habit. He never waited for inspiration. His habit was the structure that produced the work, independent of his mood. Trollope's life is proof that when you treat a habit as a non-negotiable contract with your future self, the volume of your output and the strength of your identity becomes boundless.

Habits are the machinery of consistency. By mastering the Habit Loop and applying the Goldilocks Rule, the disciplined learner ensures that their daily actions are in constant, quiet service to the highest vision of who they are striving to become.

Recommended Books

The Power of Habit — Charles Duhigg
A clear breakdown of the cue–routine–reward loop that forms the backbone of lasting habits — reinforcing your message that structure shapes identity.

CHAPTER 29

Consistency as Self-Respect

"To live is to change,
and to be perfect is to have changed often."

— Cardinal Newman

onsistency is one of the most underrated forms of intelligence. It is not glamorous. It does not attract applause. It rarely looks impressive from the outside. Most people overlook it because they are preoccupied with intensity, novelty, or the emotional buzz of motivation. But the highest form of self-respect is discipline, and consistency is the visible evidence that discipline is real.

This chapter turns that conviction into a way of living—a way of showing up for yourself daily, not through emotion, but through honor, integrity, and the quiet psychology of keeping your word. You cannot expect the world to respect your commitments if you do not consistently respect your own.

The Core Mechanism: Internal Integrity

Consistency is the practice of Internal Integrity. It is the alignment between the person you say you are and the actions you take when no one is watching. Every time you set a non-negotiable standard—15 minutes of learning, one hard conversation, a workout completed—and then violate it, you diminish your internal trust. This may seem minor, but a thousand tiny violations erode self-respect into cynicism and stagnation.

Conversely, every time you honor a small commitment to yourself—the "Don't Break the Chain" principle — you compound your internal authority. You are not just building a habit; you are building an identity that believes, I am a person who does what I say I will do. This simple, daily act of truthfulness to self is the root of all confidence.

The Psychological Engine: Self-Efficacy

This sense of internal authority is a specific psychological concept called Self-Efficacy, introduced by psychologist Albert Bandura. Self-efficacy is the belief in your ability to exert control over your own motivation, behavior, and environment. It is the core belief that you can successfully execute the course of action required to produce a desired outcome.

Consistency is the engine that drives Self-Efficacy. You do not talk your way into believing you are capable; you act your way into it. Every completed habit, every non-negotiable block of work, and every successful navigation of difficulty provides Mastery Experiences, which Bandura identified as the most powerful source of Self-Efficacy. The more consistent you are, the more evidence you collect that your will is reliable. The feeling of self-respect, then, is simply the psychological reward for being reliable.

The Story of the Two Farmers

Consider the power of this quiet dedication in the story of two neighboring farmers.

The First Farmer was brilliant and had bursts of intense, passionate work. He would work twenty hours straight in one week, then take three weeks off. He relied on motivation and intensity.

The Second Farmer was steady and methodical. He did not have bursts of intensity, but he worked his fixed schedule every day, regardless of the weather or his mood. He relied on system and consistency.

At the end of the season, the second farmer's harvest was bountiful and predictable, while the first farmer's land was scattered and chaotic. The difference was not talent or passion. It was that the second farmer respected the process. He treated the land and the schedule with a humble, non-emotional integrity. He showed up for the process, and the process, in turn, produced the result. His consistency was not just good farming; it was self-respect demonstrated through action.

Consistency is the mechanism that translates the high-level philosophical commitment of your identity into the low-level, daily reality of your life. It is the courage to be boring, to show up, and to keep your promises to the only person whose respect truly matters: yourself. By doing this, you ensure that your progress is never reliant on a fleeting emotion but on the unshakeable foundation of your own character.

Recommended Books

The Power of Full Engagement — Jim Loehr & Tony Schwartz
A foundational work on managing energy rather than time. Loehr and Schwartz break down how rhythms, recovery cycles, and intentional focus create sustainable performance — aligning perfectly with your argument that energy protection is strategic, not selfish.

Peak: Secrets from the New Science of Expertise — Anders Ericsson & Robert Pool
A research-driven exploration of how mastery is built through deliberate practice—small, precise, consistent improvements applied over time. Ericsson's work reinforces your argument that consistency is not about intensity but about disciplined repetition that compounds into excellence.

Reflection Without Calendars

CHAPTER 30

"We do not learn from experience.
We learn from reflecting on experience."

— John Dewey

Reflection is one of the most essential disciplines for a life of growth, yet one of the most misunderstood. Many people imagine reflection as a rigid review process—weekly checklists, scheduled audits, and color-coded assessments. But genuine reflection is not a calendar event. It is a way of thinking, a posture of awareness, a willingness to step back from motion long enough to see yourself clearly.

Reflection is not measured in frequency. It is measured in depth.

It is the capacity to interpret your own life as it is happening. Without it, action becomes purely reactive, learning stalls at the level of recognition, and consistency is simply a mindless repetition of old habits. The disciplined learner understands that the real work happens not in the doing, but in the processing.

The Core Mechanism: Single-Loop vs. Double-Loop Learning

Harvard organizational theorist Chris Argyris identified the critical difference between two types of learning that happen during reflection:

1. Single-Loop Learning: This is corrective. It involves detecting and correcting an error within the existing rules or paradigm. For example, coffee machine broke, so I replaced the filter. (You solved the immediate problem but didn't question the system.)

2. Double-Loop Learning: This is transformative. It involves questioning the underlying assumptions, values, and frameworks that led to the action. For example, Why do I rely on coffee so much? What does my dependence on caffeine reveal about my sleep habits and stress management? (You questioned the rule itself.)

Most people only engage in Single-Loop reflection, which results in minor, temporary fixes. The disciplined learner seeks Double-Loop Learning to change the entire system. This deep reflection is how Self-Efficacy evolves into actual mastery.

The Socratic Review: Questioning the Self

Genuine, calendar-free reflection happens when you apply epistemic curiosity to your own life. This is the Socratic Review—a process of self-interrogation that moves from the obvious to the foundational. Instead of asking simple questions like, "Did I finish my to-do list?" you ask:

- Action: What choice did I make that I would not want to make again?

- Paradigm: What unexamined belief about myself or the world led me to make that choice?

- Identity: What does that action tell me about the person I am currently becoming?

This practice is the necessary friction that keeps the ego in check, reveals the true state of your discipline, and ensures your actions are in alignment with your declared purpose.

The Story of the Missed Signal

I once missed an obvious, high-leverage business opportunity simply because I was too busy. The Thin Description of the event was: I need to better manage my calendar. The solution would have been Single-Loop: book fewer meetings.

But the Thick Description came from Double-Loop reflection: I asked, Why did I choose business motion over deep thought? I realized my calendar was full because I confused productivity with importance, and I used a frantic schedule as a way to avoid the quiet, uncomfortable work of genuine risk-taking (Courage). My unexamined paradigm was: Busy equals valuable. My system was flawed.

The true lesson was not about scheduling; it was about self-worth. I used the reflection to change the paradigm, forcing myself to dedicate a full two hours a day to "unproductive" thinking and learning. That reflection, not the meeting, unlocked the next level of growth.

Reflection without calendars is a commitment to continuous self-correction. It means building in moments of intentional stillness—a five-minute pause between meetings, a focused walk at the end of the day, a single, written question before bed—to ask the deeper why. It is the daily discipline of forcing your current self to report honestly to your future self. This is how the pursuit of knowledge becomes a lifelong commitment, rather than a temporary effort.

Recommended Books

The Long View — Matthew Kelly
A contemplative call to live from purpose rather than urgency. Kelly shows how long-term thinking, quiet reflection, and interior clarity orient

the mind toward meaning — perfectly aligned with your argument that reflection is a posture, not a scheduled event.

The Discipline of Say No: Protecting Your Sovereignty

CHAPTER 31

"People think focus means saying yes to the thing you've got to focus on. But that's not what it means at all. It means saying no to the hundred other good ideas that there are."

— Steve Jobs

I f the Anti-Schedule is the architecture you build for your time, then the Discipline of Say No is the relentless security system you install to defend it. Every single day, your time, attention, and energy are the targets of a thousand external demands—from meetings and emails to social obligations and well-meaning requests for help.

Most people manage their lives by accepting every request until they physically break. They live in a state of perpetual debt to other people's priorities. The disciplined learner understands that sovereignty over their schedule is the non-negotiable foundation of growth. If you don't say no, your Attention and your Consistency become the property of the loudest voice in the room, and your L-OS collapses into a system of reaction.

The Core Mechanism: The Hidden Cost of Yes

Saying yes feels good. It provides an immediate reward of social acceptance, validation, and temporary relief from conflict. But every "yes" to a low-leverage opportunity is an inevitable "no" to a high-leverage one. The hidden cost of a thoughtless "yes" is paid in three currencies:

1. Lost Time: The direct hours taken from your Maker Schedule.

2. Lost Energy: The cognitive switching cost (Context Switching) that fragments your focus and makes Deep Work impossible.

3. Lost Integrity: The erosion of your Self-Respect when you commit to something you resent or cannot fully deliver on.

The disciplined learner applies a Paradigm Shift: they treat their time and focus as their most finite, sacred resource. The decision to say no is not an act of arrogance; it is an act of courage and stewardship of their life's purpose.

The Tool: The Filter of Purpose

You cannot rely on emotion to say no. You must rely on a system. The most effective filter is your L-OS Purpose Statement. When a request comes in, the disciplined learner does not immediately ask, Do I have time? They ask:

1. Does this align with my primary Work, Worship, or Service? (If not, the answer is immediately no.)

2. Is this a high-leverage application of my specific skill set? (If it could be done by someone else, the answer is no.)

3. Does accepting this violate an existing boundary for Deep Work or Rest? (If yes, the answer is a firm no.)

This process ensures that your "no" is not arbitrary; it is an algorithmic decision rooted in your non-negotiable values. This makes the rejection less emotional for you and less personal for the recipient. You are not rejecting the person; you are rejecting the task based on a pre-established commitment to your highest purpose.

The Story of Peter Drucker's Focus

The management theorist Peter Drucker was famous for his radical discipline of saying no. His protégé, Joseph Maciariello, once described how Drucker would routinely refuse to participate in projects or groups that were considered mandatory for someone of his stature. His mantra was: "Only the things that are important will ever get done."

Drucker understood that every opportunity, even a "good" one, was a potential distraction from the "great" work he was designed to do. He protected his focus by treating his time as a fixed asset and his reputation for saying no as a tool of integrity. Because his boundaries were clear and consistent, people knew when they approached him that they had to bring a request that was truly high-leverage. His refusal was not a slight; it was a testament to his profound respect for the value of his own time and attention.

The Discipline of Say No is the constant, quiet maintenance of your personal sovereignty. It is the commitment to the long-term vision of your identity over the short-term pleasure of acceptance. By defending your boundaries, you defend your focus, your energy, and your entire L-OS, ensuring you have the time and clarity to complete the work you were called to create.

Recommended Books

The Art of No: Reclaim Your Power, Protect Your Purpose — Kyle Brookes
A direct, practical guide to boundary-setting. Brookes shows how saying no preserves clarity, protects energy, and keeps your commitments aligned with what matters most — exactly the message this chapter drives home.

VIII

TECHNOLOGY, AI, AND THE MODERN LEARNER

This final thematic section is dedicated to applying the fully formed L-OS in the modern age of acceleration. It establishes that technology is not a neutral force but pure amplification, making the disciplined more powerful and the distracted more fragmented. The core principle introduced is AI as Leverage: understanding that the true power of artificial intelligence is not in replacing human thought, but in becoming a 10x multiplier for a mind already trained in Synthesis and Attention. This demands the mastery of strategic input, turning Prompt Engineering into a new form of mental craftsmanship. Crucially, this section addresses the moral dimension by defining The Ethics of Attention, which requires the disciplined learner to deploy their newfound competence and leverage with integrity, ensuring their power is used for service, not manipulation.

The section culminates in the final synthesis of the book's framework. It formally presents the Learner's Operating System (L-OS) as the complete, universal structure for lifelong growth and then introduces The Architect's Mind, which demands the holistic application of all L-OS principles to the entire life structure—not just the career. This shift ensures that discipline is used to design a life built on strong foundations of health, relationships, and enduring purpose. By mastering these final disciplines, the learner ensures their framework is structurally sound, future-proof, and capable of generating value and legacy in the most chaotic, technologically advanced environment in human history.

CHAPTER 32

AI as Leverage: The Multiplier of the Disciplined Mind

"Technology is a useful servant but a dangerous master."

— Christian Lous Lange

Every generation encounters a force that reshapes what is possible. In previous centuries, it was the printing press, the steam engine, electricity, the microchip. Today, that force is artificial intelligence. But while AI feels new, the question it raises is ancient:

Will you master the tool, or will the tool master you?

AI is pure amplification. It magnifies whatever it is given. It makes the disciplined more disciplined. AI won't replace you. But the person who knows how to ask a deep, specific question will replace the person who still prompts, 'Write about business.' The machine doesn't forgive generic input. It makes the unfocused more unfocused. It multiplies direction or accelerates drift. For the disciplined learner, AI is not a replacement for thinking—it is the ultimate form of leverage.

The 10x Multiplier: The Disciplined Mind's Advantage

In the world of technology, a common ideal is the "10x Engineer"— an individual whose superior skill and insight allows them to produce ten times the output of an average peer. AI instantly turns every disciplined learner into a potential 10x thinker.

AI does not think; it processes. It does not discern; it organizes. It is a powerful prediction engine. But its output is only as valuable as the input and the discernment of the person using it.

If you feed AI with a shallow, vague, or distracted question, you get a fast, generic, and shallow answer. You have merely outsourced your drift. If you feed AI with a deep, precise, and high-quality question— forged by curiosity, guided by purpose, and checked by humility — you receive a profound, accelerated insight. The value of the tool is directly proportional to the quality of the mind wielding it.

Prompt Engineering: The New Mental Craftsmanship

The core skill of the modern learner is no longer just knowledge acquisition. It is Prompt Engineering—the art and science of formulating a question that maximizes the utility of the AI. Prompt engineering is simply Mental Craftsmanship applied to the machine.

A disciplined learner knows that a vague prompt like "Write about business" yields noise. A craftsman's prompt looks like this: "Using the principles of Level 5 Leadership (Collins) and Antifragility (Taleb), draft five bullet points on how to structure a Q3 failure report for a B2B SaaS startup. Use a tone of humble, strategic urgency."

This kind of prompt relies on the learner's existing "lattice work of mental models" and forces the AI to synthesize knowledge from multiple domains. The learner is not having the AI do the thinking; they are leveraging the AI to do the synthesis and heavy lifting of organizing their existing superior knowledge.

The Story of the Two Strategists

Consider two strategists in a high-stakes environment, both with access to the same generative AI tool:

Strategist A (The Consumer): Treats the AI like a magical answer box. They ask, "What is our Q4 strategy?" and paste the generic output into a document. They save time, but they have produced a brittle, unoriginal plan that fails at the first sign of friction. They have outsourced their thinking.

Strategist B (The Disciplined Mind): Treats the AI like a high-powered research assistant. They first spend an hour in Double-Loop Reflection to clarify their core assumptions. Then they use the AI to: 1) Synthesize the latest market data. 2) Identify the top three counter-arguments to their plan. 3) Draft a Premeditatio Malorum scenario for their team to debate. They are leveraging the AI to stress-test and sharpen their own superior strategy.

The result is that Strategist B creates a robust plan that is structurally sound and antifragile. They win, not because they used the AI more, but because they thought more deeply and asked better questions—turning the AI into a multiplier of their own pre-existing discipline.

The future belongs to the disciplined learner because they are the only ones equipped to truly master the new tools. When you master your attention, refine your focus, and strengthen your identity, AI becomes the powerful engine that carries your life's work to heights others cannot imagine. To live beneath your design in the age of AI is to choose irrelevance; to live in alignment with your design is to choose boundless leverage.

AI & Ethics

The creation of this book reflects a partnership between human discipline and modern tools. Artificial Intelligence served as a co-pilot—an accelerant for structure and clarity—but never a replacement for the work itself. Across roughly 250 hours, 2.5 years, and nineteen revisions, every idea and argument was shaped through deliberate effort, judgment, and lived experience.

Amazon now allows authors to disclose whether AI contributed to a manuscript, though that information is not shared with readers. This mirrors a long-standing tension in publishing: ghostwriting has quietly shaped a large portion of the literary world for decades (in some genres reaching well over 70 percent), especially in memoir, business, and self-help. Contributors remain invisible because the publishing model treats "author" as a brand rather than a collaborative role.

AI intensifies this tension. Ghostwriting once meant human craftsmanship; now it can mean algorithmic assistance—fast, scalable, and difficult to detect.

A personal example illustrates the complexity. Under the band name Chasing Scars, I release music on Spotify and other platforms. Much—though not all—of that catalog is created with AI tools. The journey began with a deeply personal experiment: writing a love song for my wife, Those Green, Green Eyes. What started as affection became a hobby, then an exploration of creative possibilities, and eventually a sustained curiosity about what these tools can produce—instrumentation, melodies, and lyrics.

Yet I hold a deep respect for art and the lifelong craftsmanship behind it. That respect is why AI experimentation raised difficult questions, especially when I discovered there is no way for platforms like Spotify to disclose which tracks are AI-generated. Listeners cannot tell, and creators cannot voluntarily identify their use of AI. In music, contributors are usually credited because copyright requires it; in books, ghostwriters remain hidden by design. AI now sits between these two traditions, blurring the lines further.

This leaves us with unresolved questions that every creator and platform will eventually have to address:

1. Should AI transparency follow the music industry's model of mandatory crediting or the book industry's model of silent

collaboration—and what ethical responsibilities come with each?

2. What honesty, integrity, and morality require when a machine meaningfully shapes a creative work, even if disclosure is not legally or commercially expected?

3. How do we uphold the dignity of human creativity—its intention, sacrifice, and meaning—while still embracing AI as a legitimate tool for experimentation and expression?

These questions do not yet have clear answers, but they will shape the ethics of creative work in the years ahead.

AI provides leverage. Integrity provides direction.

Next up, we continue this conversation, moving from the mechanics of AI to the ethical posture required to use it wisely.

Recommended Books

The Age of AI: And Our Human Future — Henry Kissinger, Eric Schmidt, Daniel Huttenlocher
A strategic look at how AI changes thinking, leverage, and human capability — supporting your argument that tools amplify disciplined minds.

The Ethics of Attention: Integrity in the Age of Leverage

CHAPTER 33

"Integrity is doing the right thing, even when no one is watching."

— C.S. Lewis

As the disciplined learner masters their Attention, develops their L-OS, and begins to use high-powered tools like AI as Leverage, a new, crucial discipline emerges: Integrity.

Leverage is pure amplification. It magnifies the good in your purpose or the flaw in your character. In an age where one person with a focused mind and a powerful tool can create the output of a small team, the moral and ethical intent of that one person is the single greatest determinant of the tool's impact. The question shifts from Can I do this? to Should I do this?

The Ethics of Attention is the commitment to ensure that your focus, competence, and leverage are directed toward Service, not manipulation, hoarding, or self-aggrandizement.

The Core Mechanism: The Integrity Gap

In the age of leverage, a gap emerges between Competence and Character.

- Competence: What you can do (your skill, your AI proficiency, your knowledge).

- Integrity: What you choose to do with that competence (your alignment with truth, honesty, and purpose).

The integrity gap is created when a person uses their heightened skill to pursue a shallow or dishonest end. They have the L-OS, but their moral operating system is corrupt. This is the ultimate danger of the modern learner: a highly efficient, focused mind directed by a brittle, selfish purpose.

The antidote is the daily practice of checking the source of your actions. Integrity is not a one-time decision; it is the Consistency of choosing the virtuous path, even when the dishonest path offers greater short-term rewards.

The Ethics of Information

The disciplined learner treats information itself with ethical rigor. When using tools like AI, the ethical standards of the L-OS demand that you:

1. Own the Output: Never use the AI's speed to obscure the truth or avoid the difficult work of original thought. Your name is on the work, and your character is its source.

2. Honor the Source: When you synthesize knowledge, you honor the Great Conversation by citing your sources, acknowledging your mentors, and giving credit where it is due. The humble learner knows their knowledge is borrowed, not generated.

3. Resist Manipulation: Use your understanding of psychology and attention to build value, not to exploit vulnerabilities or perpetuate the noise that leads to the modern condition.

The Story of the Two Programmers

Consider two expert programmers who discover a novel, highly efficient security flaw in a common, widely used software system.

Programmer A (High Competence, Low Integrity): Uses the flaw for private financial gain. They see the skill as a license to exploit, prioritizing short-term profit over the foundational principle of service. Their leverage harms thousands of passive users.

Programmer B (High Competence, High Integrity): Immediately and anonymously reports the vulnerability to the company. They use their knowledge—their highest form of leverage—to secure the system and protect the collective. They see their skill as a calling for Service and stewardship.

The difference in action was not in their technical ability; it was in their character. The disciplined learner understands that the greatest return on their education is the ability to choose the principled path, regardless of the temptation of the immediate reward.

Integrity is the essential armor for the Age of Leverage. It ensures that the power of your focus is used to build a robust legacy—one that benefits others and remains structurally sound long after the technological advantage has faded. To live with integrity is to ensure your L-OS is an engine for good.

The Learner's Operating System (L-OS): A Framework for the Modern Age

CHAPTER 34

"The mind is not a vessel to be filled, but a fire to be kindled."

— Plutarch

Lifelong learning requires more than desire, curiosity, or access to information. It requires structure—a way of approaching knowledge, reflection, discipline, and growth that remains stable as the world shifts. Throughout this book, you have built the deep foundations: identity, purpose, consistency, discipline, clarity, noticing, reflection, and courage.

Now those foundations converge into a single framework:

The Learner's Operating System — the L-OS.

An operating system determines how every component of a machine interacts, processes, adapts, and performs. In the same way, the L-OS shapes how a person acquires knowledge, integrates experience, builds skill, and forms identity. It is the invisible architecture beneath growth, the structure beneath mastery, the order beneath your intellectual and spiritual life.

The L-OS consists of seven pillars—not steps, not stages, not a program. These are forces that operate simultaneously across a lifetime, guiding the learner through an age shaped by distraction, acceleration, and technological upheaval.

The Core Discipline: First Principles Thinking

The entire L-OS is built upon the ability to see reality clearly, unburdened by assumption. This is known as First Principles Thinking—a mental tool popularized by thinkers like Elon Musk but rooted in the foundational work of Aristotle. First Principles Thinking is the act of boiling every complex problem down to its fundamental truths, the core elements that you know are unassailable.

When you look at a problem—a personal failure, a complex business challenge, or a new skill—the L-OS forces you to discard analogy and assumption. Instead of asking, "How has this always been done?" you ask, "What are the physical, psychological, and economic facts at play?" This discipline, learned through a commitment to foundational truth, ensures that the L-OS is always operating from reality, not from inherited paradigms.

The Seven Pillars of the L-OS

These pillars are the synthesized, non-negotiable elements that convert passive consumption into active growth:

1. Identity (The Foundation):

Identity determines direction, and direction determines learning. This is the constant internal conviction: I am a learner. This pillar protects you from the comfort of stagnation and the paralysis of fear. It is the commitment to self-authorship.

2. Purpose (The Compass):

Your L-OS must be aligned with your vocation. This is the integrated understanding of Work, Worship, and Service. Purpose converts difficult action into meaningful effort, ensuring that your learning serves a calling larger than your own immediate self-interest.

3. Paradigm (The Lens):

This is the continuous discipline of checking your mental maps. The L-OS demands that you actively seek Double-Loop Learning and challenge the underlying assumptions that lead to behavioral or strategic errors. It is the courage to admit your map is flawed.

4. Discipline (The Energy Source):

This is the rejection of comfort and the mastery of the Prefrontal Cortex. Discipline ensures that effort is not dependent on motivation but on systematic action. It is the commitment to consistency as self-respect.

5. Attention (The Filter):

This is the rigorous defense of your focus from overstimulation and noise. Attention allows you to practice The Skill of Noticing, separating the thin data from the thick insight. You must control the inputs to control the output.

6. Synthesis (The Processor):

This is Mental Craftsmanship in action. It is the process of forcing knowledge into the internal Lattice Work through high-friction processing (like the Feynman Technique). Synthesis ensures that information becomes integrated wisdom, not just consumed data.

7. Leverage (The Multiplier):

This is the strategic application of AI and Mentorship to accelerate growth. It is the understanding that time is finite, and the fastest path to competence is a superior strategy and the use of tools to multiply your existing discipline.

The L-OS is the final structure that makes lifelong learning sustainable, inevitable, and antifragile. It is the final synthesis of the book's core argument: to live a powerful life in the modern age, you must reject the drift of convenience and design a personal operating system built for intentional growth.

Recommended Books

Ultralearning — Scott Young

A tactical guide to aggressive, self-directed learning systems — directly reinforcing your L-OS framework and the value of intentional, structured skill acquisition.

The Architect's Mind: Designing a Life, Not Just a Career

CHAPTER 35

"We are the architects of our own destiny."

— Albert Einstein

The final synthesis of the Learner's Operating System (L-OS) is the conscious realization that you are not merely managing a career; you are designing a life. The principles of the L-OS—from Paradigm Mastery to Consistency to Leverage—are universal tools. The disciplined learner applies them holistically, treating their health, relationships, and finances with the same rigor they apply to their professional growth.

The most common and destructive failure of the ambitious is Compartmentalization. They achieve success in one area—often career —while allowing the rest of their life to operate by default. They have a brilliant professional Paradigm, but a shallow or broken personal one. The result is a brittle, fragile life: an impressive structure built on a cracked foundation.

The Architect's Mind rejects this compromise. It understands that mastery is indivisible. You cannot be a disciplined learner in your career while being a reckless consumer in your health. Your attention, integrity, and focus are singular assets that must be applied to the design of the entire life structure.

The Core Mechanism: Holistic Design

Holistic design means applying the L-OS to the three non-negotiable foundations that support all long-term growth:

1. Health (The Foundation of Energy): Your physical and mental health is the operating platform for the L-OS. It is the primary discipline of Rest, Discipline, and Dopamine Reset. If your energy is low, your focus fragments, and your Maker Time is wasted. The Architect's Mind prioritizes exercise, nutrition, and sleep as high-leverage professional decisions.

2. Relationships (The Foundation of Resilience): Your tribe, family, and closest relationships are the source of Resilience and Purpose. They are the ultimate defense against the modern condition. The Architect's Mind applies the principles of Attention to their closest ties, knowing that Consistency in a relationship is the highest form of self-respect.

3. Vocation (The Foundation of Meaning): This is the alignment of your Work, Worship, and Service across the entire 168 hours of your week. It is the continuous process of Reflection to ensure your daily actions are in integrity with your life's deepest calling.

The Tool: The Three-Column Audit

A simple, high-friction tool for the Architect's Mind is the Three-Column Audit, which should be performed during periods of Reflection:

1. What is my biggest professional failure this month?

2. What is the core personal flaw that enabled that failure? (e.g., Lack of discipline, fear of conflict, poor self-talk, and exhaustion.)

3. What is the smallest, most immediate action I can take on the personal flaw? (e.g., go to bed 15 minutes earlier, write a daily journal entry, or schedule a difficult conversation.)

This audit eliminates the compartmentalized thinking that allows a personal flaw to sabotage a professional goal. It forces the learner to see the entire life structure as a single, interdependent system.

The Story of the Balanced Leader

The historian and biographer Doris Kearns Goodwin often writes about the most successful and resilient leaders in history. The leaders who sustained their integrity and purpose over decades were those who had clear, non-negotiable boundaries outside of their primary work.

They were the ones who protected their family time, who engaged in a regular, low-stakes hobby, or who maintained a consistent spiritual practice. Their non-work life was not a passive retreat; it was an actively designed source of resilience that allowed them to withstand the political, professional, and personal shocks that broke their peers. Their success was not a matter of working more hours; it was a matter of building a stronger life structure.

The Architect's Mind understands that the final product of the L-OS is not a successful career but a well-designed life. The true measure of a learner's mastery is not the accumulation of knowledge but the integrity with which that knowledge is deployed across the entire messy, beautiful structure of their life.

Building Your Personal Learning System in the Age of AI

CHAPTER 36

> *"In the long run, a short attention span makes fools of us all."*

— Cal Newport

A learning life is not built by intensity, novelty, or good intentions. It is built by structure — the kind that steadies you without constraining you. In an age shaped by AI, distraction, and relentless acceleration, the need for a Personal Learning System has never been more urgent. This system is the practical, daily expression of the L-OS.

Your Personal Learning System (PLS) is the disciplined feedback loop that converts your identity into actionable habits and your information into integrated wisdom. The aim is not efficiency. The aim is formation— to become someone who learns deeply, lives wisely, and acts with strength.

The PLS can be structured around three critical, non-negotiable stages: Inputs, Processes, and Outputs.

Stage 1: Inputs — Building an Information Diet

The first act of mental craftsmanship is the rigorous curation of what you allow into your mind. Garbage in, garbage out. The vast majority of information available today is low-value noise—easy dopamine hits that feed only Diversive Curiosity.

The disciplined learner operates on a strict Information Diet. They filter aggressively, knowing that every choice to consume frivolous content is a choice against building their mental lattice work.

- The Filter of Time: Author and Modern Stoic Ryan Holiday famously advocates for reading old books because they have passed the "ultimate filter of time." If a book has survived a century, its fundamental wisdom is likely profound, eliminating the noise of contemporary trends. The learner prioritizes foundational works over fleeting headlines.

- The Filter of Friction: Avoid frictionless, auto-playing, passive consumption. Choose books over articles, long-form essays over social media feeds, and focused thinking over instant reaction. The effort required to access high-value material is the price of admission for superior knowledge.

Stage 2: Processes — Forging Knowledge into Memory

Once information has been accepted into the system, it must be subjected to high-friction processing to convert it into usable memory. Passive reading does not create a skill; active processing does.

- Spaced Repetition and Active Recall: The most powerful tool for memorization is the principle of Spaced Repetition. This scientifically proven method involves reviewing information at increasing intervals over time, forcing the brain to engage in active recall (retrieving the answer from memory, not simply recognizing it). Modern tools like digital flashcard apps (Anki) or knowledge management platforms (Notion) are simply vehicles for this process. The technology is new, but the discipline is ancient: force yourself to remember.

- The 5-Minute Synthesis: Immediately after finishing a new concept, engage in the Feynman Technique by writing a short, personal summary of the core idea. You must articulate the new information in your own words, connecting it to a problem or a prior mental model. This is the moment of synthesis, where a fact is transformed into an insight.

Stage 3: Outputs — Testing and Leveraging Wisdom

The final stage of the PLS is the externalization of knowledge—applying it, teaching it, and testing it. This is where the wisdom becomes antifragile.

- The AI Stress-Test: AI is the perfect partner for this stage. Instead of using it to generate an answer, use it to challenge your answer. For example: after synthesizing a new strategy, prompt the AI: "Identify the three most critical flaws in this strategy based on principles of behavioral economics and historical precedent." The AI acts as a relentless, unemotional Devil's Advocate, forcing you into Double-Loop Learning and immediately checking your humility.

- Service and Teaching: The ultimate output is Service. When you teach a concept to someone else, you are forced into the ultimate act of synthesis and simplification. The clarity required to help another person understand a complex idea ensures that you yourself have truly mastered it. Service is the final proof that your PLS is working—that you have created value not just for yourself, but for the world.

Building a Personal Learning System is the essential act of self-sovereignty in the age of distraction. It is the decision to live by design, not by default. By mastering your Inputs, applying high-friction Processes, and using powerful Outputs, you ensure that every day, you go to bed smarter, clearer, and more capable than when you woke up.

PART

IX

CONCLUSION

CONTINUOUS JOURNEY

Thus final section is the definitive launch point for the entire Learner's Operating System (L-OS). Having constructed your internal foundation, built the mastery disciplines, and armed yourself with the ultimate leverage, the final necessary step is to move from theory to creation. This conclusion rejects the modern impulse to wait for perfection, clarity, or permission. It shifts the entire focus from learning for self-improvement to learning for contribution, affirming the highest purpose of the disciplined mind is to generate value for the world. This is the moment where the work of Identity is proven, and the commitment to Service is realized.

The final chapter, "Create Anyway," serves as the ultimate call to action and the book's final synthesis. It grounds the entire process in the conviction that creation is not a hobby reserved for the gifted but a calling woven into the soul of every human being. By choosing to build, write, speak, or teach—even when you are scared, uncertain, or incomplete—you honor your purpose and begin to shape the future. The conclusion is a final, simple, and powerful directive: the world has enough spectators; the future belongs only to the disciplined learner who is willing to create.

Create Anyway: Why Ordinary People Build Extraordinary Things

CHAPTER 37

"Look beside you and find the creators,
for they are the ones shaping the future."

— G. K. Chesterton

Most people never create anything—not because they lack intelligence, resources, or opportunity, but because they believe creation belongs to someone else. Someone wealthier. Someone more gifted. Someone who has it all figured out.

But here's the truth, and it's the reason this final chapter exists: You don't need extraordinary success to create something meaningful.

I say that as a man who has built some good things, failed at others, kept learning, kept grinding, and kept showing up. The single thread running through all of it is this: I chose to create anyway. And you can, too.

It's about courage. It's about identity. It's about creative obedience. And it's about the simple truth that ordinary people change their lives—and sometimes other people's lives—by taking creative risks long before they feel qualified.

Creation doesn't belong to the elite.

It belongs to the willing.

Made in the Image of a Creator

Let's start here, because this sits at the core of how I see the world: Human beings are made in the image of a Creator.

This is not a philosophy; it is a profound biological and spiritual fact. You are designed to create. This is your fundamental nature, and to ignore it is to suppress your own purpose. You were made to work, to design, to shape, to contribute, to bring something into existence that did not exist before.

When you ignore that creative instinct—when you suppress the impulse to build, write, speak, teach –something in the human soul wilts. You feel restless, cut off from meaning. Your creativity is not an optional upgrade; it is your birthright. The pursuit of learning is the discipline that honors your design.

The Only Necessary Qualification

I have never been a member of the world's elite. I do not own a global empire. I don't have unlimited resources. I've done well, but my level of success has never determined my level of creativity. And neither should yours.

Creativity isn't a reward for "making it." Creativity is a choice you make before you "make it."

If I had waited until I was wealthy, or widely known, or operating with perfect clarity and perfect confidence, this book wouldn't exist. Perfect conditions never come. Confidence never arrives fully formed. Clarity is something you gain while you move—not before.

The world is full of people far wealthier and far more successful than I am who have never created a single meaningful thing. Wealth doesn't make creators. Willingness does.

My Crossroads: The Purpose of Leverage

One of the defining moments of my life came during a season when I had two small businesses and the pressure of a family depending on me. Money was painfully tight. I faced a choice: Take a stable, predictable job, or burn the ships and bet on myself.

The stable path was sensible. The creative path was dangerous. But I knew that if I surrendered to safety, I would lose the part of me that believed in possibility.

So I locked myself in a room for a week. I hired a tutor. And I learned. Until my brain hurt. Until the ideas clicked.

That week didn't make me wealthy. But it changed everything. It taught me that learning is the ultimate leverage. It taught me that if I didn't learn to create when everything was uncertain, I would never create when things became stable.

That moment required courage and obedience to the creative impulse inside me. My ultimate purpose is to help people, because that is what I believe I am designed to do. This book is a direct application of that conviction. If this book is a complete commercial flop, but it helped just one person find their purpose of helping people, it was worth it.

Stop Waiting to Be Ready

People delay creativity because they think the right moment will reveal itself. They think confidence will settle in. You will never feel fully ready. You will never feel fully qualified. You don't create because you're ready. You create because you're called.

Called to steward the gifts you've been given. Called to speak into the lives of others. Called to contribute something good.

Read this carefully: The world doesn't need your perfection. It needs your contribution. In the age of AI, your creation is not limited by your technical skill but by the depth of your question and the courage of your will. Use the tools, but own the vision.

Write the Book. Record the Podcast. Start the Business. Make the Thing.

Do it poorly at first. Do it nervously. Do it while you're still learning. Do it even if only a handful of people will ever see it.

Your Life Doesn't Need to Be Perfect—You Just Need to Move

This book teaches you the entire Learner's Operating System (L-OS): identity, purpose, discipline, systems, focus, and courage. The final step —the one that turns all of that into something real—is simple: Create.

The L-OS is the engine. Creation is the output.

Create even when you're scared.

Create even when you don't feel successful.

Create anyway.

The world is not shaped by the perfect.

It's shaped by the willing.

A Call to Action |

I f you forget every line in this book except one, let it be this: The disciplined learner is always a creator.

You need courage.

You need systems.

You need a purpose rooted in service.

Go honor the image of the Creator stamped into your soul.

Write.

Speak.

Build.

Teach.

Make.

Begin.

The world has more than enough spectators.

What it desperately needs is more creators.

Creators like you.

RESOURCES FOR THE LIFELONG LEARNER

P eople learn differently. Some absorb information slowly and deeply. Others learn rapidly and make connections across topics. Some prefer books, while others learn best through discussion, hands-on practice, or watching others. There is no universal method that works for everyone.

The more you practice the art of learning, the more you understand how you learn. Learning is a skill—one that sharpens with repetition, experimentation, curiosity, and exposure. Over time, patterns emerge, your preferences become clearer, and you discover the tools and methods that help you grow the fastest.

These are some of the resources and practices that have helped me most in my own lifelong learning journey. They are organized into the three practical stages of the Learner's Operating System (L-OS) to help you structure your approach. -----I. High-Leverage Input & Capture

This section focuses on the disciplined acquisition of high-quality information, ensuring your consumption feeds your knowledge lattice, not your distraction habit.

1. Audible and Speed Learning

Audiobooks are one of my primary learning tools, and over the years, I trained myself to listen at speeds most people think are impossible— 2.5x to 3x, depending on the narrator. This didn't happen naturally. It happened through intentional practice designed to push the limits of my comprehension. This method is a real-world application of the discipline of Challenge, deliberately forcing your brain to engage its capacity for neuroplasticity—the brain's ability to adapt and strengthen under controlled stress.

Here's the method:

1. Identify the speed at which you're comfortable. If that's 1.2x, start there.

2. Push far beyond your comfort zone. Set your audiobook to 2.0x or even 2.5x for five minutes. It should feel uncomfortably fast. Your brain will be working hard, but it adjusts quickly.

3. After five minutes, reduce the speed—but not back to your old comfort zone. If 1.2x was comfortable, drop down only to 1.4x.

Your comprehension will catch up faster than you expect. Do this for the first ten minutes of whatever you listen to each day. Push well above your limit, then settle slightly above your previous comfort level. Repeat this daily, and your baseline speed will rise steadily.

This technique works across multiple platforms, not just Audible:

- Podcasts
- YouTube videos
- Training videos
- Online courses
- Short-form content
- Recorded lectures

2. Blinkist and Shortform

Not every book needs to be read cover to cover. Sometimes you just need the core insights or a quick overview before deciding whether to commit to the full text.

- Blinkist condenses books into short summaries you can read or listen to in ten to fifteen minutes.

- Shortform expands on summaries with commentary, cross-referencing, and deeper analysis.

These tools are excellent for rapidly exploring new subjects or previewing a book before diving in. They're not replacements for full reading, but they're powerful accelerators for Diversive Curiosity leading to Epistemic Curiosity.

3. Podcasts

Podcasts make it easy to turn otherwise idle time into learning time. Driving, exercising, doing yard work, cleaning—any low-focus activity becomes an opportunity to grow. And the same speed-learning principles apply. Speed them up. Train your brain to handle more input. Podcasts offer access to some of the world's sharpest thinkers and experts and are one of the most flexible and high-value learning tools available.

4. YouTube Lecture Playlists

Universities, professors, and experts release full lectures and series for free. Creating curated playlists around subjects you're studying can become your own self-designed curriculum, allowing you to build foundational knowledge without distraction. -----II. High-Friction Processing & Synthesis

This stage is the Mental Craftsmanship of the L-OS, where consumed information is forged into integrated wisdom.

A. Digital Note-Taking Systems: The Synthesis Engine

Tools like Notion, Obsidian, and Evernote allow you to capture ideas, outline insights, save quotes, build summaries, and create a personal knowledge library. Learning compounds when you store and revisit what you study. These systems are essential for the high-friction work of Synthesis, enabling you to physically connect concepts from different sources and build The Lattice Work of mental models. -----III. Accountability, Leverage, and Community

This final stage is the application of knowledge, the testing of paradigms, and the commitment to growth through collective accountability.

1. ChatGPT: The Multiplier of the Disciplined Mind

AI is one of the greatest learning accelerators we've ever had. With the right Prompt Engineering, you can transform this tool into a high-powered thinking partner and Devil's Advocate.

With AI, you can:

- Break down complex ideas
- Create study guides
- Compare concepts across multiple authors
- Build learning plans
- Tutor you through difficult subjects
- Expand perspectives quickly

The key is to treat AI as a thinking partner—not a replacement for thinking. When used well, it multiplies your learning capacity.

2. Online Courses

When you need depth and structure for a specific skill, online courses are incredibly effective. They provide step-by-step guidance and focus in ways that books and podcasts sometimes can't, providing the sequencing necessary for rapid skill acquisition.

Strong platforms include:

- Udemy

- Coursera

- MasterClass

- Skillshare

- LinkedIn Learning

3. CodeTap

CodeTap is one of my companies, created to help people adapt AI into their business life with clarity and purpose.

If you run a business or lead a team and want to integrate AI into your workflow, CodeTap provides tools and guidance to help you:

- Build systems around your daily work

- Automate repetitive tasks

- Improve speed, clarity, and output

- Use AI in planning and strategy

- Turn your existing knowledge into usable, repeatable workflows

If you want to bring AI into your business in a practical, structured way, CodeTap is designed to make that process easier and more effective.

CodeTap.ai

4. Reading Groups and Mastermind Circles

Tools are powerful, but people shape you more. Discussion deepens understanding. A small group reading one book a month—or even one book a quarter—helps clarify ideas, test assumptions, and sharpen thinking. This is the peer-level mentorship that accelerates growth. Community accelerates learning.

5. Iron Oak Society

If you are a man looking for accountability, challenge, brotherhood, and growth, the Iron Oaks Society is worth exploring.

Iron Oaks is built on commitment, responsibility, and the pursuit of becoming better men—stronger husbands, fathers, leaders, and learners. I serve on the board, and I've seen firsthand how transformative it can be when men surround themselves with others who refuse to settle. A strong community sharpens you in ways no app or tool ever could.

IronOakSociety.com

ACKNOWLEDGMENTS

I must take this moment to thank the learners in my life:

To my parents for giving me the tools for an amazing life filled with wonder, purpose, and an orientation toward God.

To my incredible wife, Ashli, thank you for being my unshakeable foundation, my first and best editor, and the truest example of dedication and grace. Every word of this book was written with your support.

To my children [too many to list by name], you inspire me daily to never stop exploring, questioning, and growing. You are the "why" behind the continuous learning I preach.

To my friends, who encouraged me to pursue more, be better, and to write the damn book.

It is time to get to work. Be willing to accept the friction, be willing to challenge the map, and be willing to grow into the person you were created to be.

— Chase Powell